Leon Hicks:

Iconic Caper/Dancing

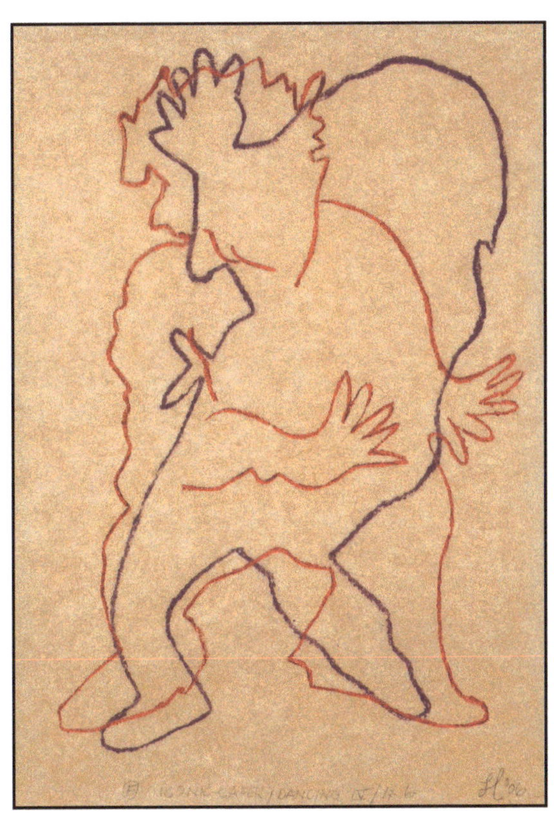

Essay by Olivia Lahs-Gonzales

The Sheldon Art Galleries, St. Louis

Leon Hicks: Iconic Caper/Dancing
Is published by the Sheldon Art Galleries, St, Louis
in conjunction with the exhibition in the
Bellwether Gallery of St. Louis Artists, Sheldon Art Galleries
February 24 - June 30, 2007
The exhibition and catalogue are made possible by Kenneth and Nancy Kranzberg

ISBN: 978-0-6151-4101-5

Lulu ID: 611725 (www.lulu.com)

Cover Image:
Leon Hicks, *B Iconic Caper/Dancing III #2*, 2006. Courtesy of the Artist and Three Sinks Gallery, Webster Groves, Missouri.

Frontispiece Image:
Leon Hicks, *F Iconic Caper/Dancing IV*, #6, 2006. Courtesy of the Artist and Three Sinks Gallery, Webster Groves, Missouri.

The Sheldon Art Galleries
3648 Washington Boulevard
St. Louis, MO 63108
Telephone: 314.533.9900
Website: www.sheldonconcerthall.org/galleries.asp

Iconic Caper/Dancing

Printmaker, virtuoso draughtsman, theoretician and Professor Emeritus in the Art Department at Webster University in St. Louis since 1999, Leon Hicks has for over 50 years created works that are at once aesthetically beautiful and conceptually complex. Though he has studied and been inspired by Albrecht Dürer, Rembrandt van Rijn, Pablo Picasso, Henri Matisse, his teacher Mauricio Lasansky and more broadly, by African art and Asian calligraphy, Hicks has also embraced contemporary artistic and scientific theory and practice in his work.

Born Leon Nathaniel Hicks on Christmas Day in 1933, he already had the unique soul of an artist when he graduated from Lincoln High School in Gainesville, Florida in 1953. (His contribution to the commencement celebrations — the creation of a painting on stage during the commencement exercises — could be considered his first "performance art" piece). After a three-year tour in the army, Hicks went on to study painting at Kansas State University, where he received a B.S. degree in painting and sculpture in 1956. He received an M.A. degree in painting in 1961 and an M.F.A in printmaking in 1963 from the University of Iowa, where he studied with Lasansky. He continued his studies at Stanford University in 1964, reading ancient and modern art history. In 1966, he attended La Romita School of Art, studying Italian art history and culture. It was during this time that he used his savings to travel to Italy to immerse himself in the history and techniques of the master artists and the architecture of Assisi, Orvieto, Florence, Sienna, Rome and other cities. He began his teaching career in 1964 at Florida A&M University, where he taught for one year. From 1965, he taught for three years at Concord College (now University), Athens, West Virginia; three years at Lincoln University, Jefferson City, Missouri and four years at Lehigh University in Bethlehem, Pennsylvania before coming to Webster University in 1974. A beloved and inspiring teacher, he remained at Webster University until his retirement to Florida in 1999.

Though he resisted categorization as an "African-American" artist, in the 1960s Hicks embraced the Black Art movement, seeing this artistic imperative as a statement of solidarity for and commitment to the civil rights movement. "My participation," wrote Hicks, "had many implications. Primarily, it meant that my artworks would be rejected by the mainstream...however, I am proud of these artworks because they corroborate the practice of my cultural heritage, and they express the collective perceptions that go along with experiencing and being a black American. Even more, in the African-American community, these artworks aid in the social struggle to neutralize the stigma of historical American servitude. These artworks also are a direct "spiritual catharsis" which extended the distance between the life one lives and the art that expresses it."[1] In 1971, to enhance his own work within the Black Art movement, he took courses on African-American art history at Atlanta University. It was also during this period that Hicks established Hicks Etchprint, Inc., in Philadelphia, a company that has helped both African-American and white artists access the marketplace. Today, the Hicks Etchprint Company provides scholarships to students in the names of artists who have had distinguished careers.

In his Black Art period, Hicks created a series of iconic "Africanesque" portraits in multicolored intaglio. Initially hoping to capture a kind of universal black iconography that encapsulated "ethnic iconic concepts," he later rejected this initiative as too constricting. Realizing that he "did not have to represent all black people," he began to move away from figurative imagery and concentrated on integrating new developments in science and technology into his work.

In this transitional period, which developed throughout the 1970s, Hicks' work evolved into an exploration of formal elements, coupled with concepts that considered and deconstructed ideas, theories and concepts relating to computer science. The exhibition *Programmed Visuals* of 1979 elucidated his interest in these emerging concepts of computer technology and their influence on society. With a series of 40 engravings, Hicks let the study of plane and analytical geometry and the new language of computer programming be the catalyst to a new vocabulary of patterns, textures and shapes that might express the language of the times. "Computers were the underlying foundation," Hicks explained. In this group of engravings, Hicks was interested in the "positive aspects of technology... the input and output...."[2] He had already acknowledged the importance of the viewer in the creation of the overall experience of his works of art in past installations and the same was true for this body of work. "I am the engraver," Hicks explains; however he also feels that the viewer must complete the experience. "It's in your eye... art will always be visual... the subject is incidental."[3]

In addition to his studies of the techniques of great master artists like Rembrandt or Picasso, Leon Hicks has been interested in alternative and non-traditional methods of display. His earliest experience with installation art came after his sojourn in Italy when, in 1970, he produced *Baroque Transformation*, an installation-based exhibition at Lehigh University in Bethlehem, Pennsylvania, where he taught from 1970 to 1974. *Baroque Transformation* was also exhibited in a modified form at Webster University in 1982. These "environmental installations" as Hicks terms them, engage the viewer as "performer" in the piece, making them critical to the experience and interpretation of the whole. This has been true of many recent installations that Hicks has mounted, including his monumental suite of 31 prints from 1996 titled *Virtualscape*, exhibited at Webster University in 1996 and at five other university galleries between 1996 and 1998. Prints from this series are in the collections of the Saint Louis Art Museum and Fisk University, among others.

Keenly aware that the viewer brings their own set of ideas, expectations and responses to the art, Hicks enthusiastically integrates this element of chance into his works. He relinquishes control easily after completing his part in the process, which in the case of the Sheldon Art Galleries exhibition *Iconic Caper/Dancing* involves the creation of a series of drawings lettered and numbered in the order in which they were made. Still relevant in this body of work is his description of an earlier installation in which he "extends the development of aesthetic structures for human experience and perceptions as they are modified by mental and physical (bodily) schema."[4] Hicks' artistic ideas stem from wide readings in art history, technological advances in computer technology, philosophy, and contemporary art theory. In his proposal for the 1996 *Virtualscape/Installation* at Webster University's Hunt Gallery he quotes Terry Gips, who wrote in an article on computers and art that the "deconstruction of information is not just an activity of the Postmodernist intellectual; its lessons have seeped into society at large. Electronic technologies facilitate the production and distribution of information; more pictures, words and sounds reach more people. Simultaneously, more people participate in this process, learning to understand the complex layers of meaning in all texts — including pictures — and the relationships between texts, their creators and their consumers."[5] Hicks responded to these ideas with the installation *Virtualscape*. With the exhibition, Hicks asked the audience to be an observer-performer rather than a passive observer. Kept intentionally free of any references, the abstract prints were meant to engender a myriad of experiences and interpretations from the viewers and this result formed the final work of art.

For each of his exhibitions, Hicks also prepares complex theoretical proposals which analyze and illuminate the way in which the works are meant to function in relation to the viewer. Since the late 1970s, his interest in "Generative Aesthetics" — a term, proposed by the German philosopher and theoretician Max Bense, for a process-fed system of aesthetic structure in which operations, rules and theorems are created to explore materials, techniques and formal elements, resulting in a final structured series — has been at the heart of many of his installation projects.

In Hicks' most recent installation at the Sheldon Art Galleries in St. Louis, he employs a similar system of Generative Aesthetics, combining it with his interest in dislocating the singular artistic voice of the artist. *Iconic Caper/Dancing*, presents a new body of work conceived as a celebration of dancing and expressive movement. While teaching at Florida A & M University, where students actively engage in hip-hop dance, Hicks was first inspired to create a series of drawings titled *The Hip-Hop Allegories*. A fan of opera and its themes, Hicks saw parallels to what he termed the "operatic beat" and universality of life's rituals, in his students' hip-hop dance moves.[6] He sees dance as a unifying expression that can be carried across cultures and ethnicities, and hip-hop has certainly bridged cultures internationally.

With roots in West Africa, the Caribbean and North America, hip-hop grew from street parties in New York City in the 1970s. The sounds of funk, disco and soul were transformed by disk jockeys who manipulated two record turntables with an audio mixer to produce new and more danceable music. As hip-hop developed, the spoken word became more important. In addition to manipulating existing sounds, new compositions were created, which incorporated rhyme and beat along with social and political messages. Hip-hop continued to gain popularity in the 1980s and 90s and has spread worldwide into the new Millennium as far Japan, which has its own distinct hip-hop culture.

The exhibition *Iconic Caper/Dancing* is composed of a selection from three series. The larger group of drawings from the series *Iconic Caper/Dancing* emerged from an earlier series titled *The Hip-Hop Allegories* which are smaller, finely detailed, atmospheric ink on paper drawings that in their scope and execution have the epic qualities of Picasso's *Vollard Suite*. Hicks used individual figures from *The Hip-Hop Allegories* to generate simplified stencil matrices for the dancers in *Iconic Caper/Dancing*. Creating rubbings from stencils made from sandpaper on transparent rice paper, Hicks used grease pencil and Rembrandt pastels to define the dancing figures. The final drawings with simplified dancing forms are hung in the gallery from a wire hanging system so that they move and undulate with atmospheric conditions and the passing of the viewer.

In *Iconic Caper/Dancing* Hicks is also keenly aware of the presence and the action/reaction of the viewer. He presents his installations as a total experience rather than as a collection of independent works of art that are meant to be experienced as such. It is this "interface" between the viewer and the work that is critical to Hicks' realization of the final work. Enthusiastically discarding traditional artistic concepts of authorship and the individuality of the artist in the 19th and early 20th century concept of the word, Hicks allows others to participate in the execution of the final work. When finished with his drawings for *Iconic Caper/Dancing*, Hicks turned over the pieces and allowed the exhibiting institution to create the final installation sequence based on guiding notes from the artist.

In addition to the audience collaboration that is so integral to Hicks' work, another group of related drawings in the exhibition incorporates artistic collaboration of a different kind. In the group of drawings titled *Three Sinks X Series, Iconic Caper/Dancing: Special Series*, Hicks asked fellow artists to contribute to the pieces by printing the names of hip-hop artists onto the drawings with hand carved stamps.[7] Using names that Hicks provided, they gathered on New Year's Day, 2007 at Three Sinks Gallery in Webster Groves, Missouri, to carve the stamps and implement this collaborative element.

In the exhibition, the drawings from *Iconic Caper/Dancing* and "*...X Series...*"were paired with a group of drawings from *The Hip-Hop Allegories*. These pen and ink drawings from 2005 were installed in a grid at the entrance to the exhibition to complement and play off of the more simplified forms in the later works. Playful, airy and beautiful, Hicks' installation of the distilled and iconic drawings of *Iconic Caper/Dancing* and their more elaborate counterparts found in *The Hip-Hop Allegories* series evokes the universal energy and language of dance and the poetry of movement. This body of work continues and elaborates on Hicks' career explorations of the rich function and capacity of artistic expression and serves to create a bridge between historical traditions and contemporary practices.

Olivia Lahs-Gonzales, Director
The Sheldon Art Galleries

Biography

Leon Hicks has a M.F.A degree in printmaking and an M.A. in painting from the State University of Iowa and a B.S. in painting and sculpture from Kansas State University. He also studied Art History at Stanford University, La Romita School of Art, and Atlanta University. Hicks has exhibited nationally and internationally at numerous institutions including Miami University, Oxford, Ohio; Alabama State University, Montgomery, Alabama; University of Hawaii, Hilo and at the United States Embassy, Ankara, Turkey, among others. His works are in the collections of the University of Iowa, Iowa City, Iowa; Charleston Art Gallery, Charleston, West Virginia, Oakland Art Museum, Oakland, California; the Saint Louis Art Museum, Saint Louis, Missouri and the Library of Congress, Washington D.C., among others. His work is published in *Directions of African-American Art*, Herbert F. Johnson Museum, Ithaca, New York, *Who's Who in American Art* and numerous other publication and has been reviewed in *Art News* and the *New Art Examiner*. He was recipient of the prestigious Missouri Arts Award in 2000 and was made Professor Emeritus upon his retirement from Webster University in 1999. Leon Hicks is represented by Three Sinks Gallery in Webster Groves, Missouri.

End Notes:

1. Leon Hicks, "Personal Statement: Leon N. Hicks (Artist, 1992)," unpublished manuscript, 1992.
2. From "Programmed Visuals" in *Webster University Journal*, January 26, 1979, and Nancy Nottonson, "I am an Engraver" in *Webster University Journal*, February 1, 1979.
3. Ibid.
4. Leon Hicks, Exhibition Proposal for *Virtual Landscape Installation*, (final title *Virtualscape / Installation*) at Webster University, March 20, 1994.
5. Terry Gips, "Computers and Art: Issues of Content," *Art Journal*, Fall 1990, pp. 229-232, as quoted by Leon Hicks in his exhibition proposal *Virtual Landscape Installation*, March 20, 1994.
6. Conversation with the artist in December, 2006.
7. The contributors to the *Three Sinks X Series* were Liz Streeter, Catherine Enslin, Michelle Moran, Bridget Hilgeman, Russ Miller, Steve Stacy, Lisa Campbell, Julie Campbell and John Ahearn.

Leon Hicks: Iconic Caper / Dancing was shown in the Bellwether Gallery of St. Louis Artists of the Sheldon Art Galleries from February 24 to June 30, 2007.

The exhibition and catalogue are made possible by Kenneth and Nancy Kranzberg

Iconic Caper/Dancing

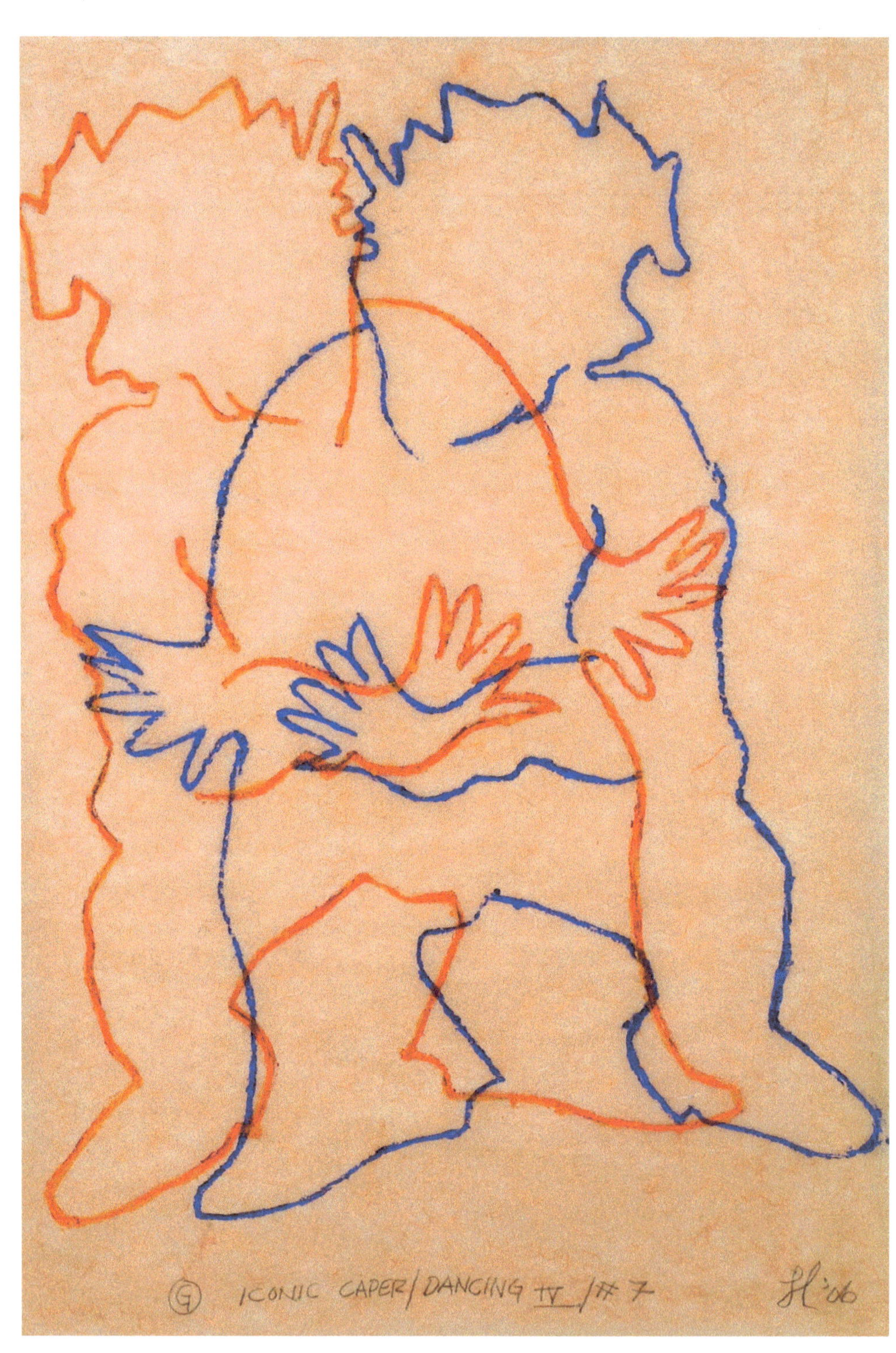

G Iconic Caper / Dancing IV, #7, 2006

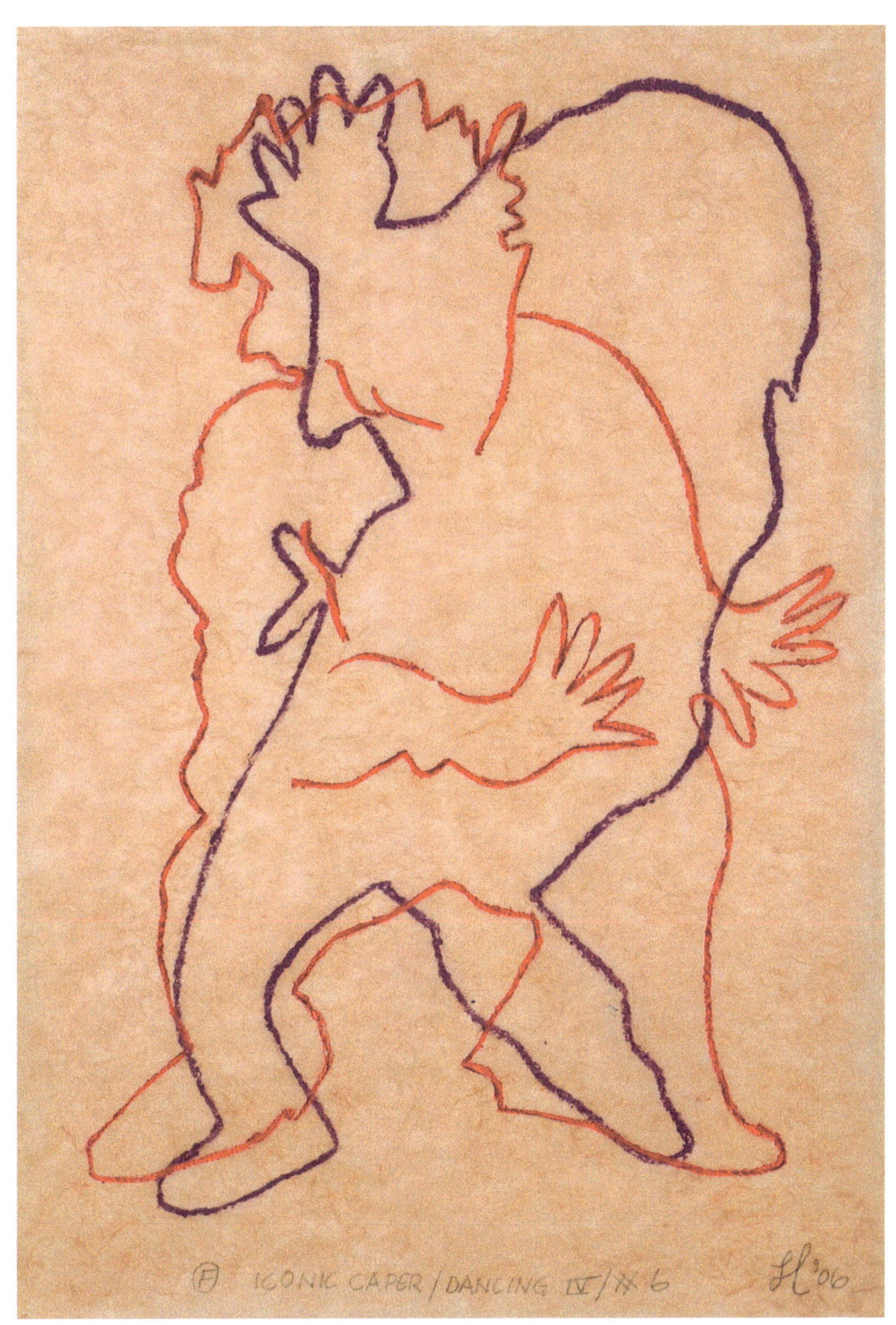

F Iconic Caper / Dancing IV, #6, 2006

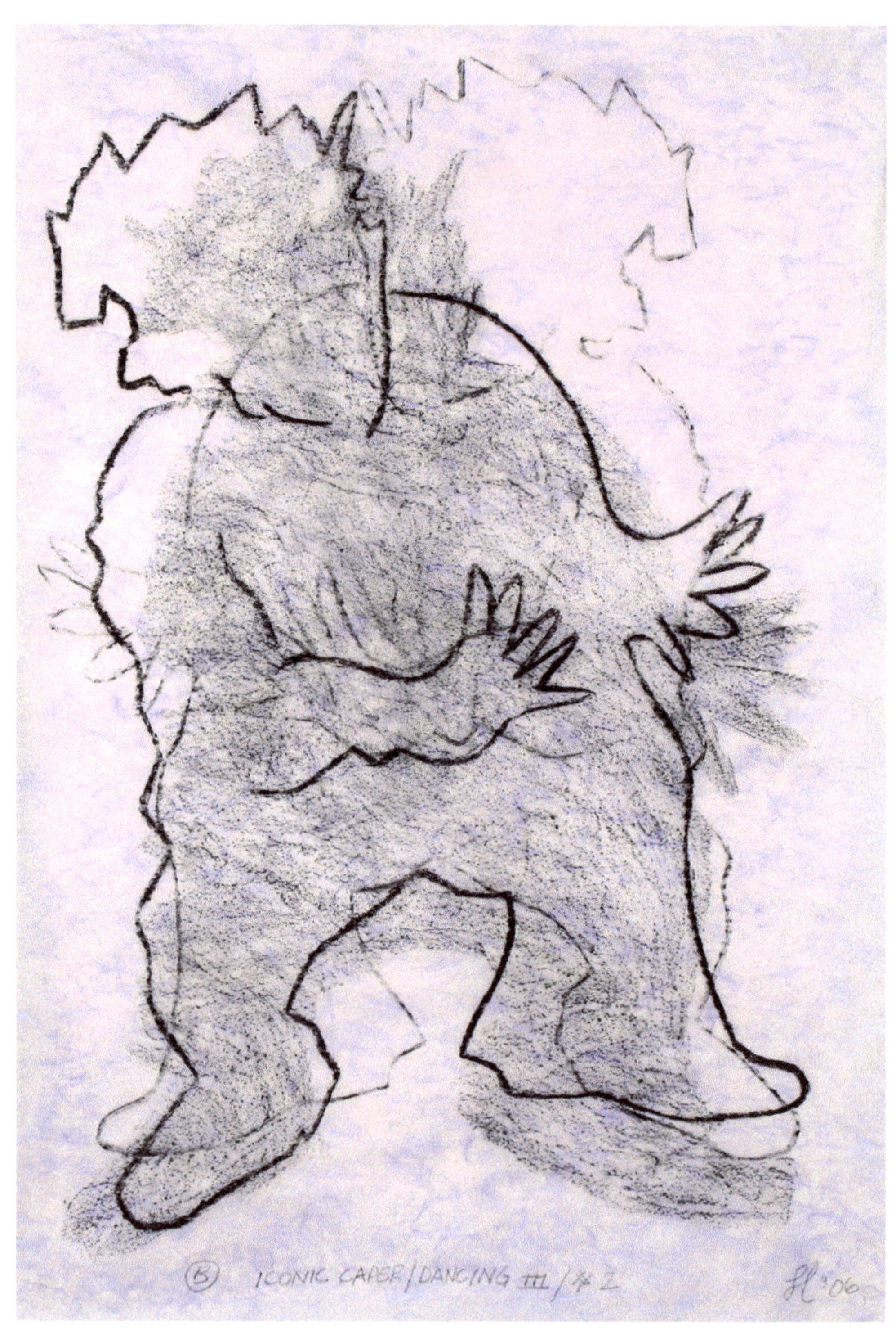

B Iconic Caper / Dancing III, *#2*, 2006

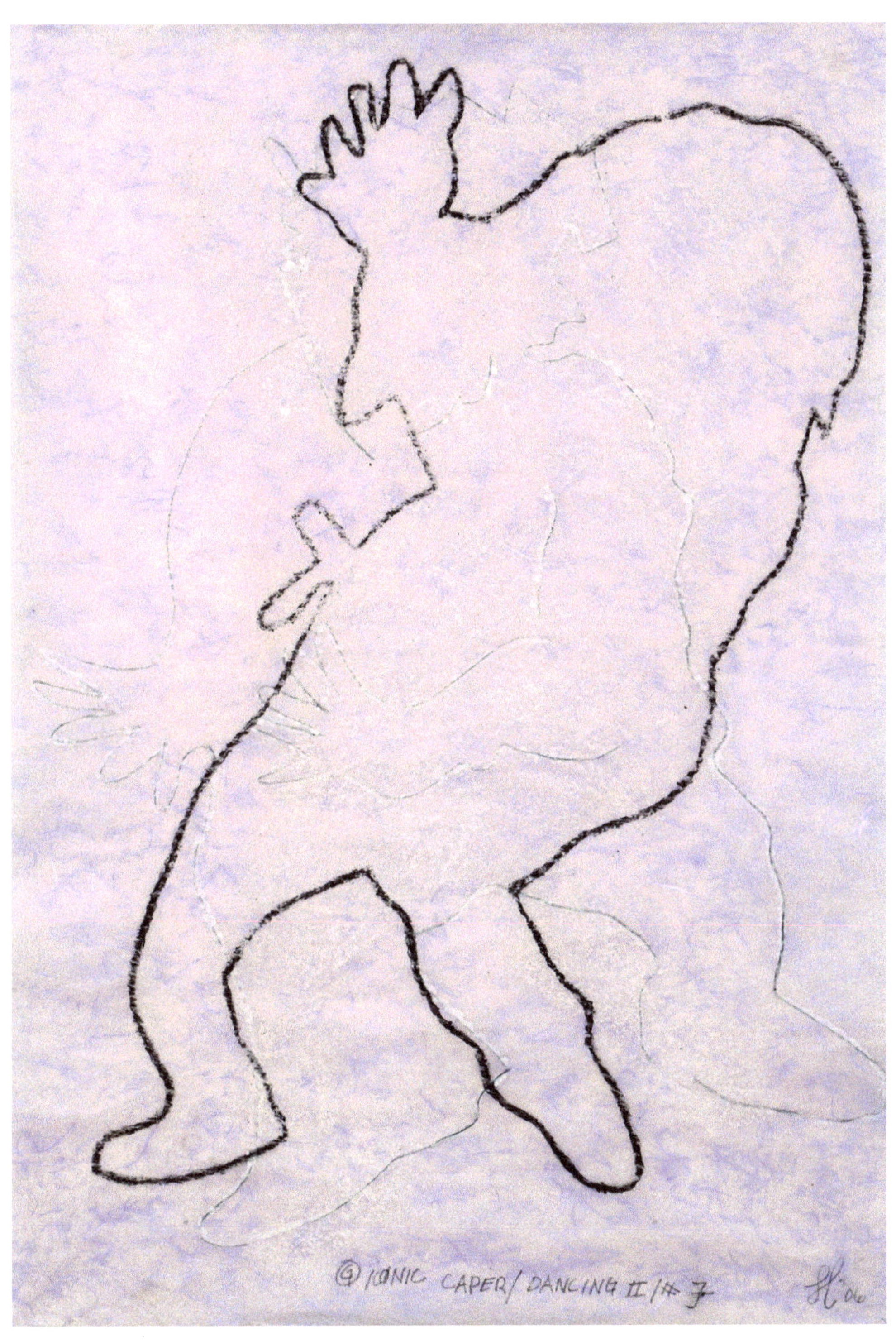

G Iconic Caper / Dancing II, #7, 2006

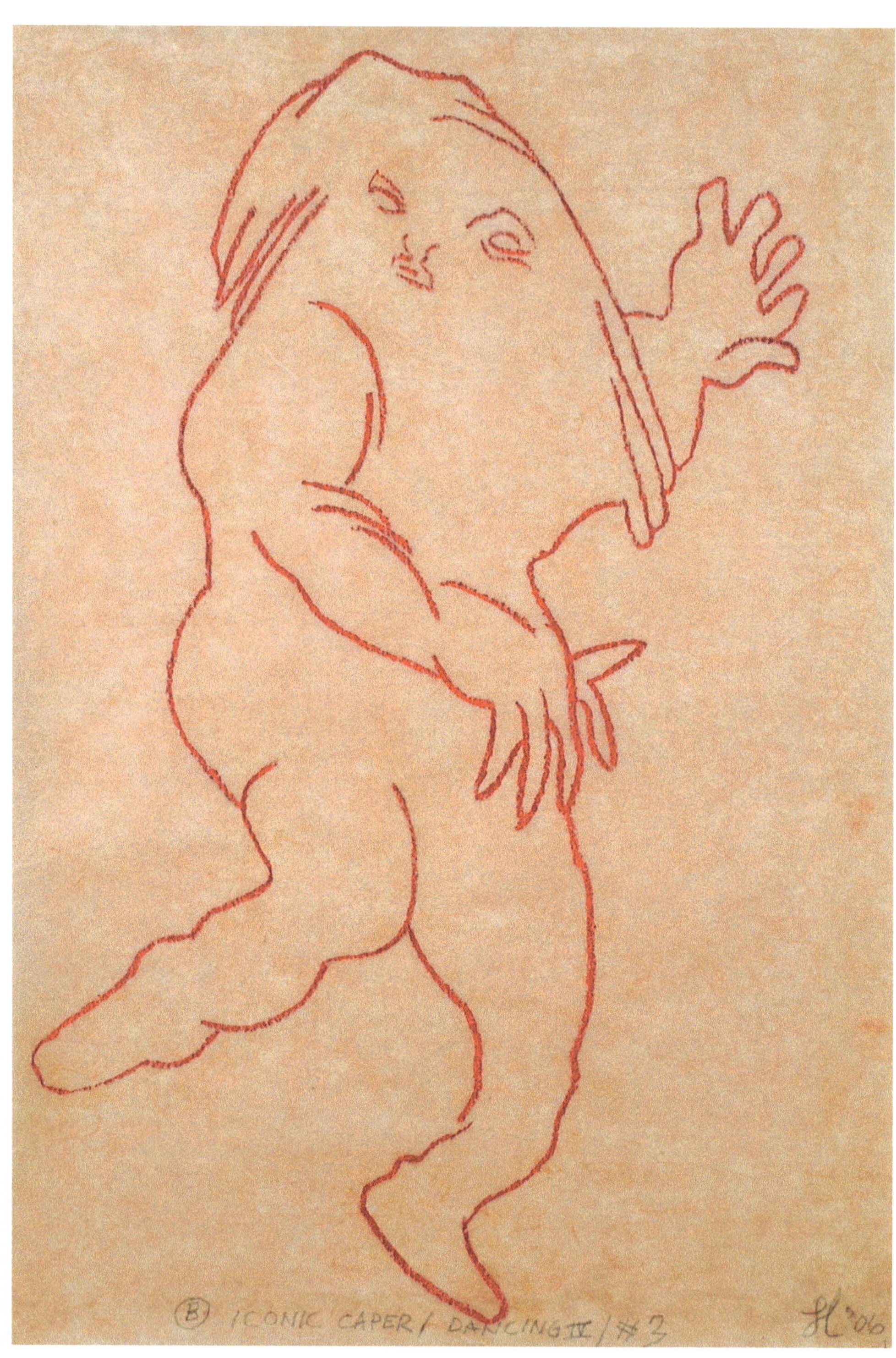

B Iconic Caper / Dancing IV, #3, 2006

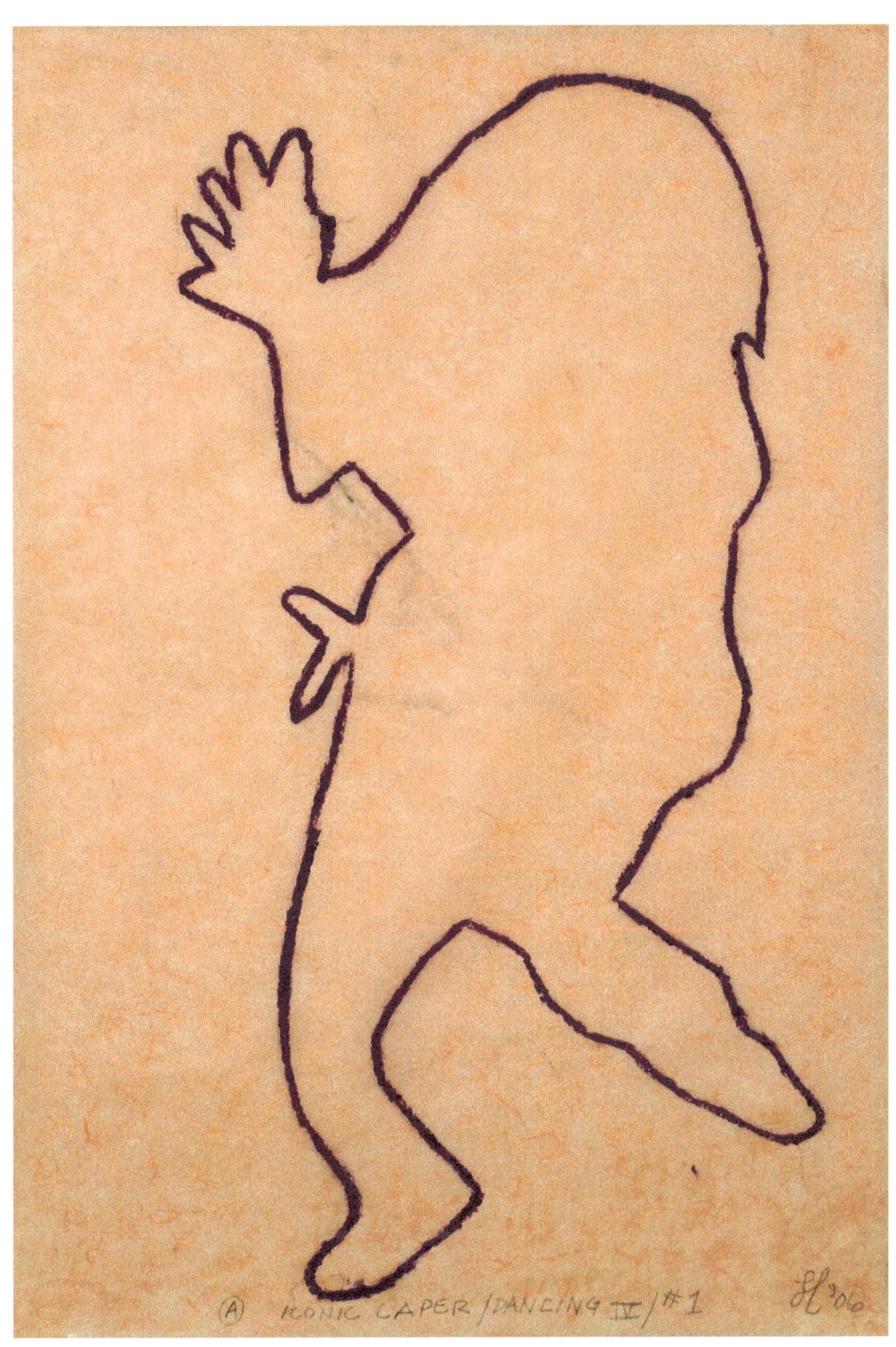

A Iconic Caper / Dancing IV, #1, 2006

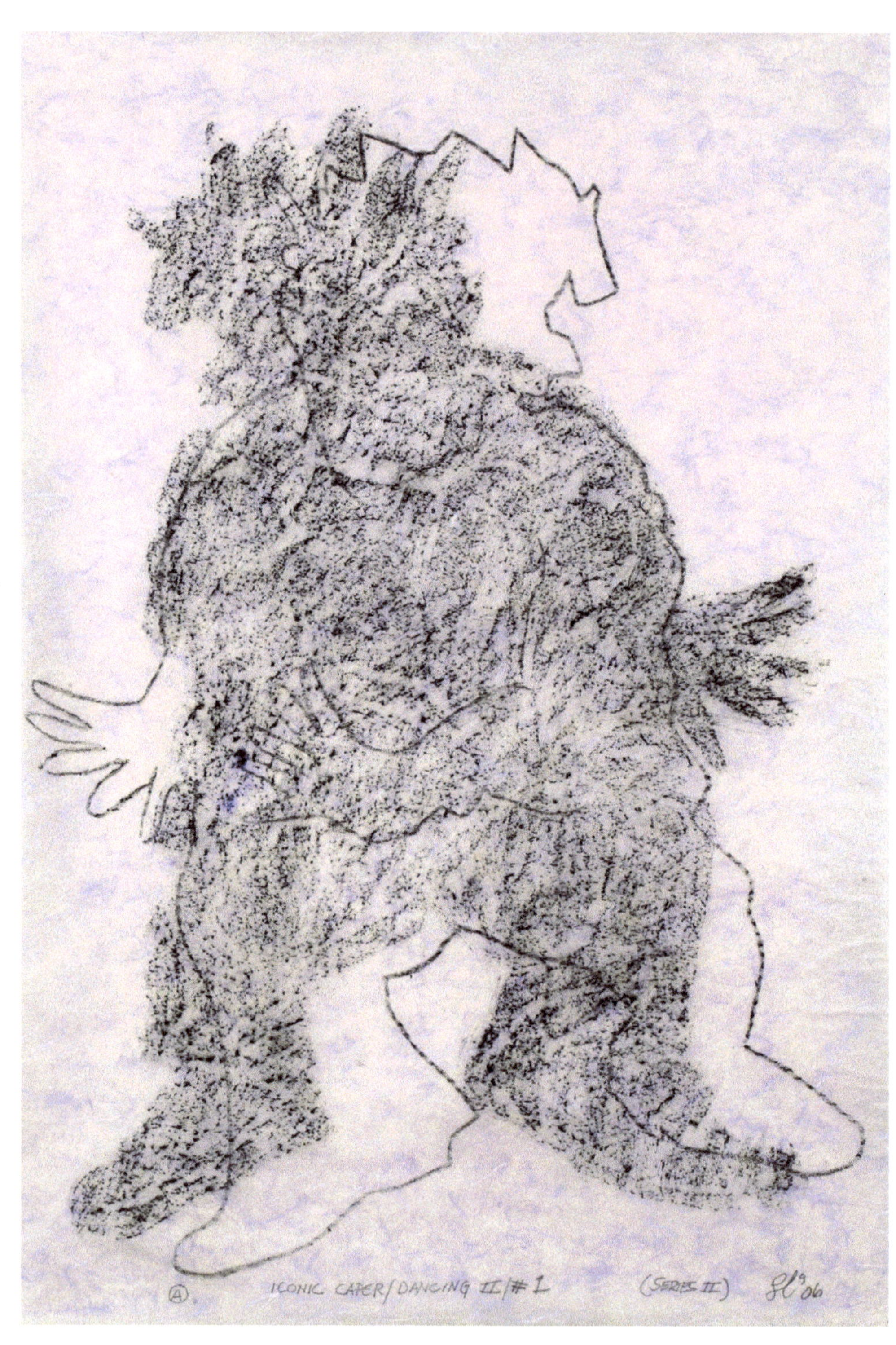

A Iconic Caper / Dancing II, #1, 2006

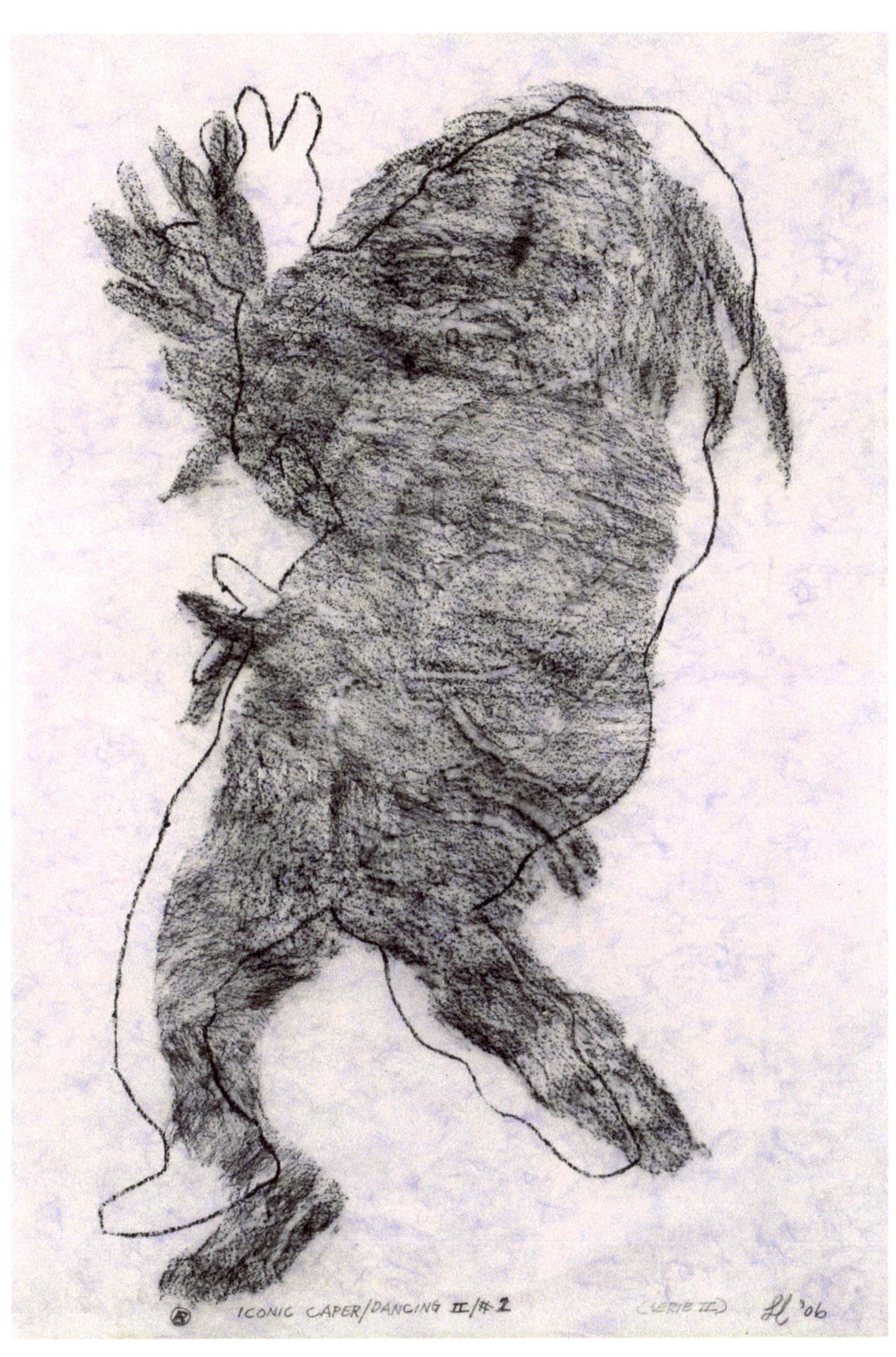

B Iconic Caper / Dancing II, #2, 2006

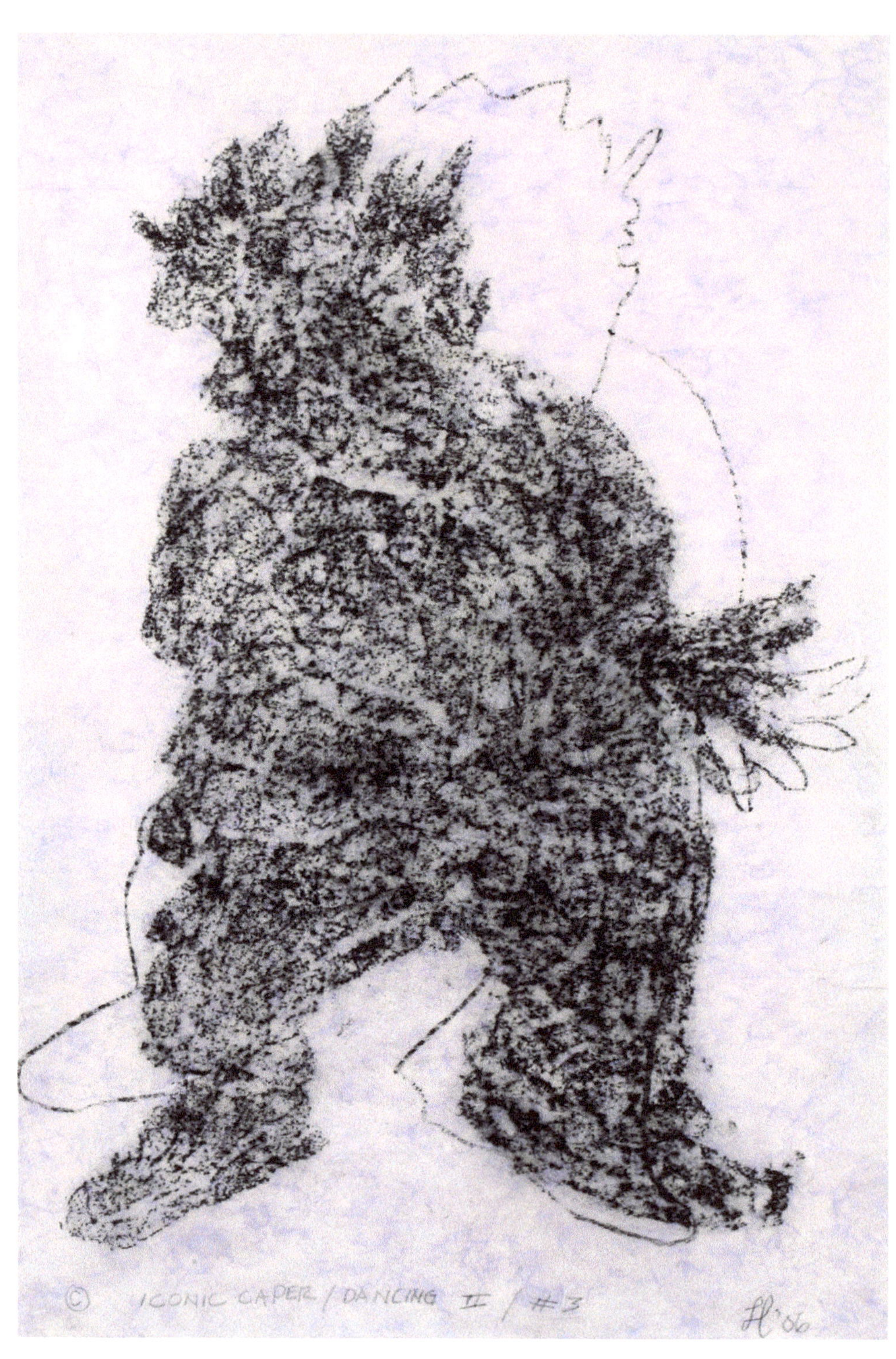

C Iconic Caper / Dancing II, *#3*, 2006

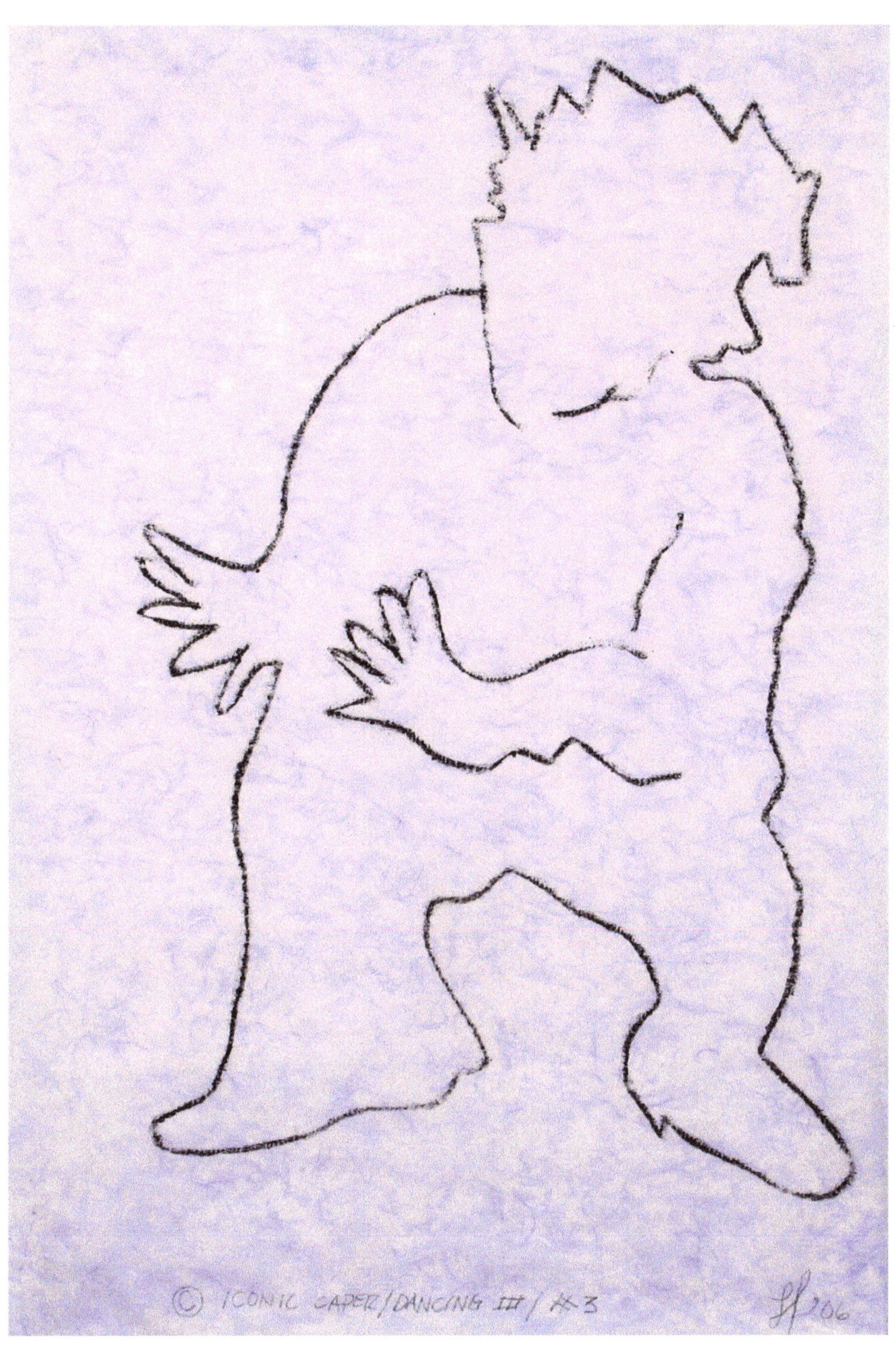

C Iconic Caper / Dancing III, #3, 2006

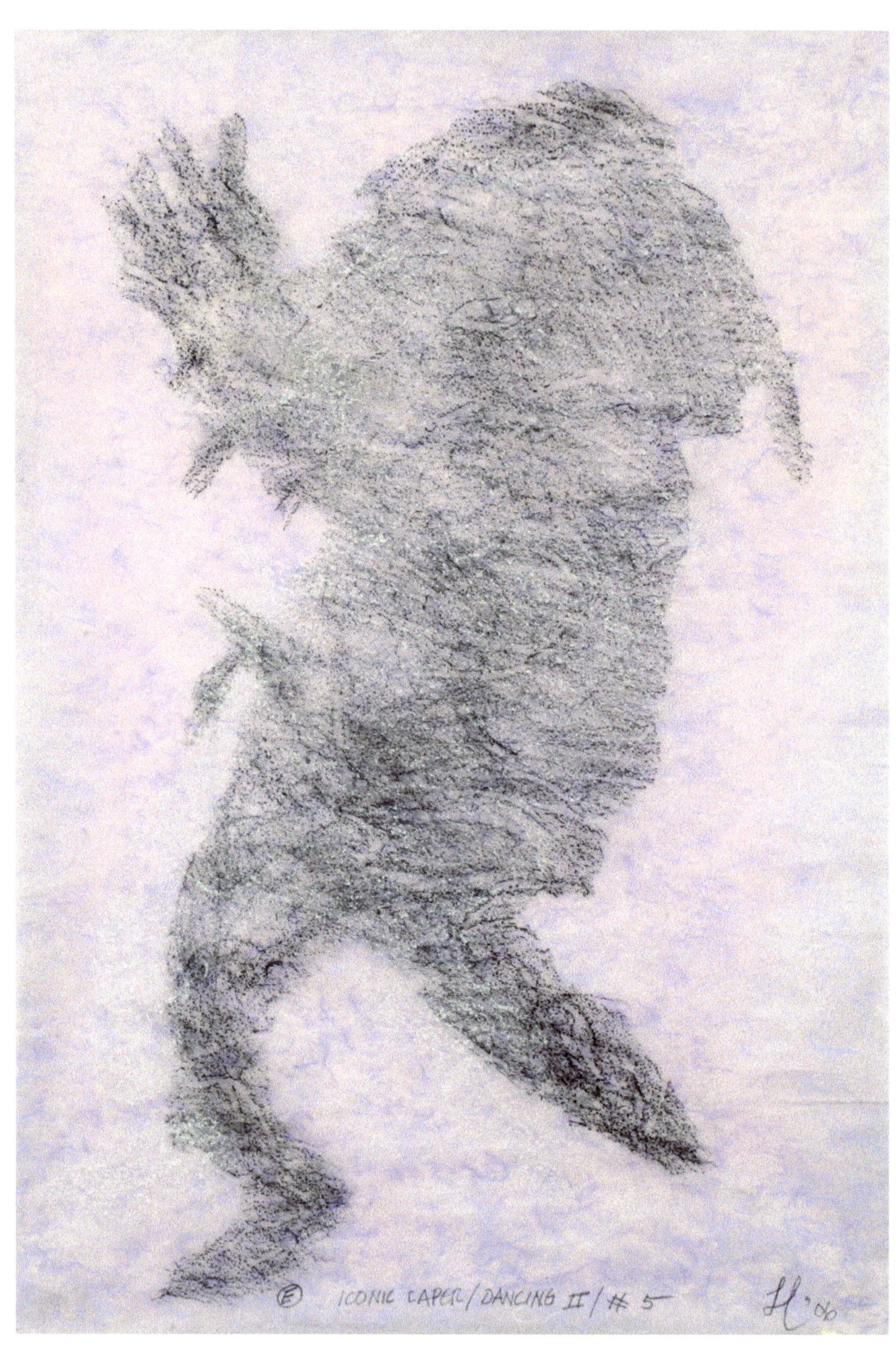

E Iconic Caper / Dancing II, #5, 2006

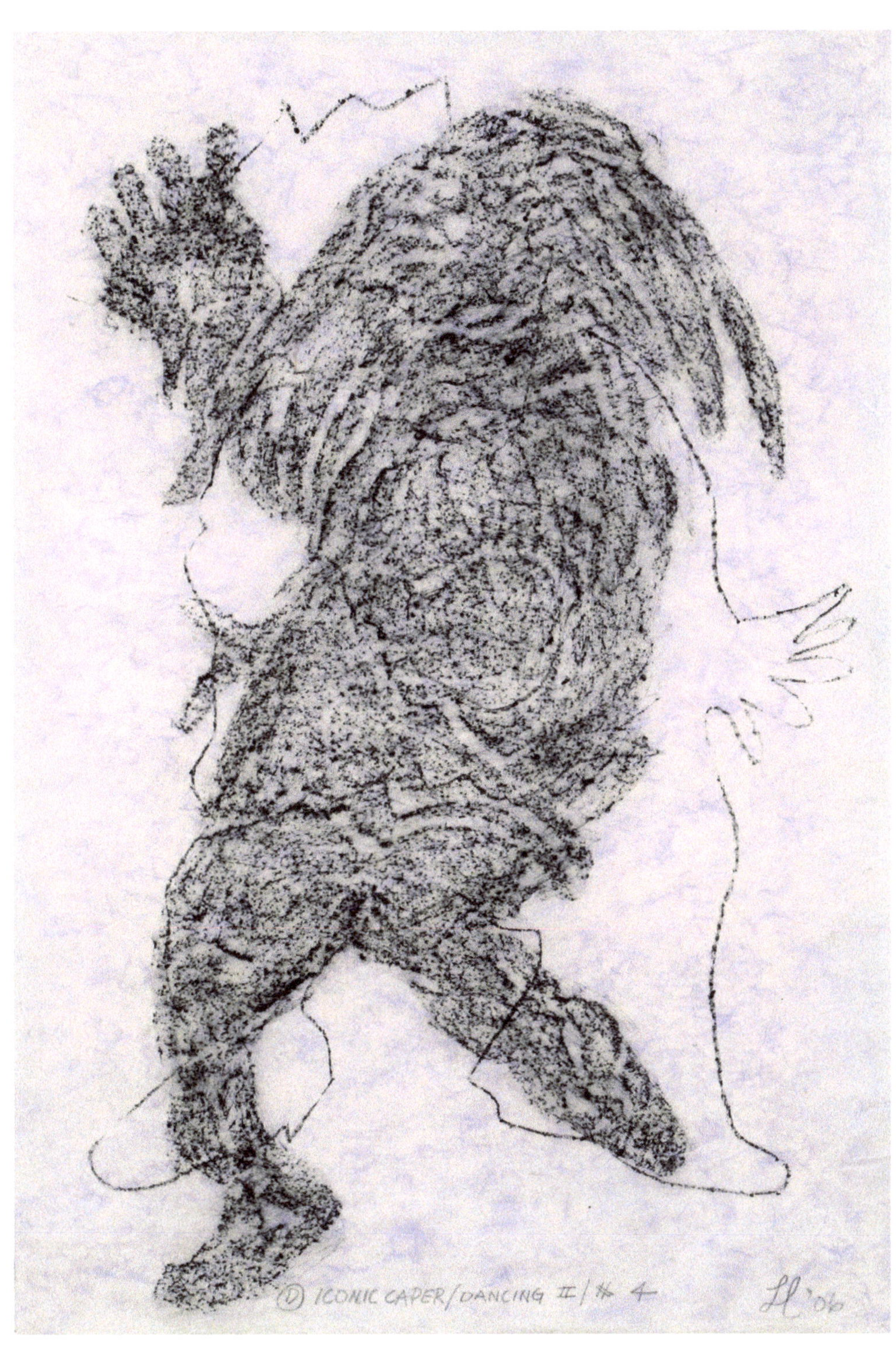

D Iconic Caper / Dancing II, #4, 2006

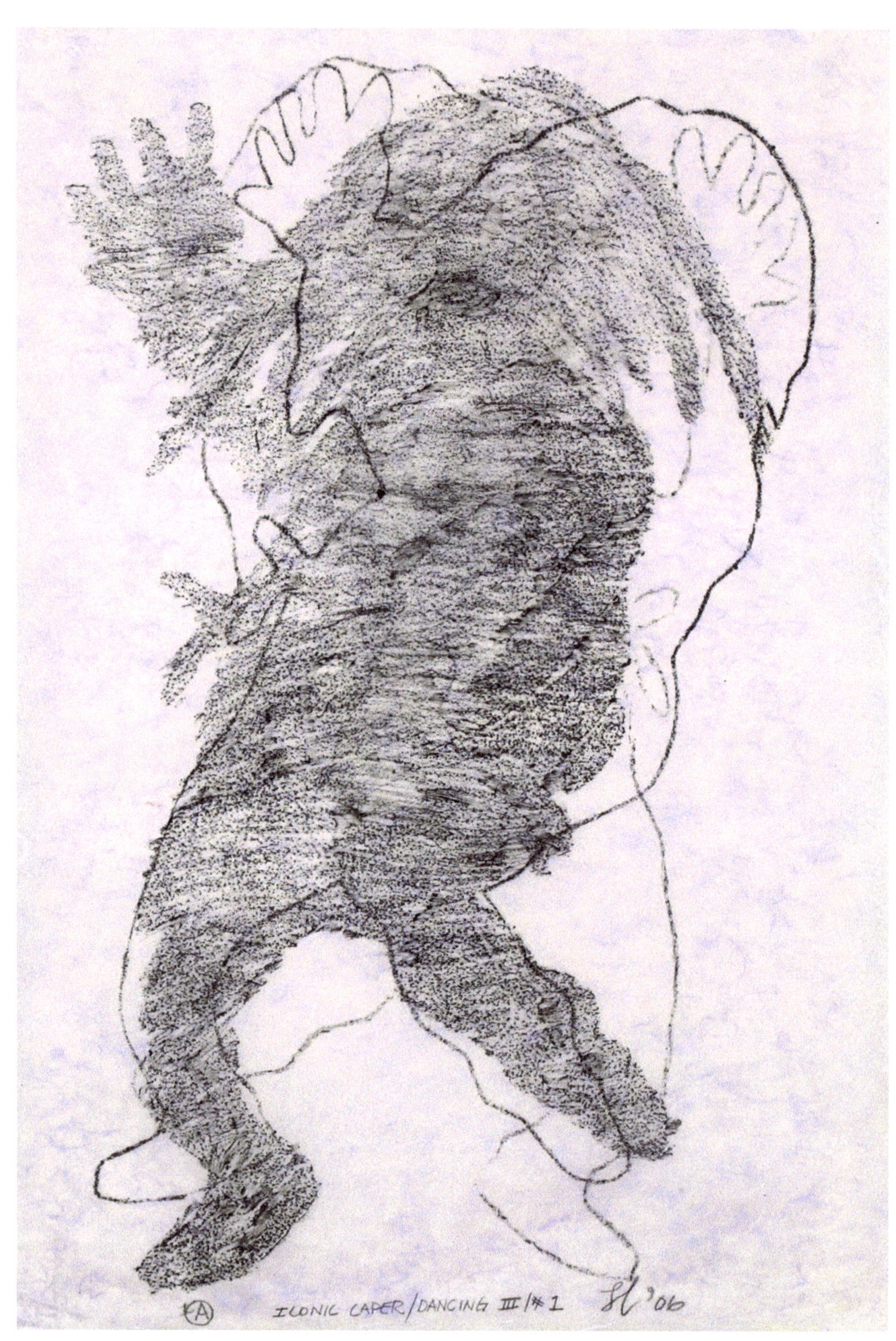

A Iconic Caper / Dancing III, #1, 2006

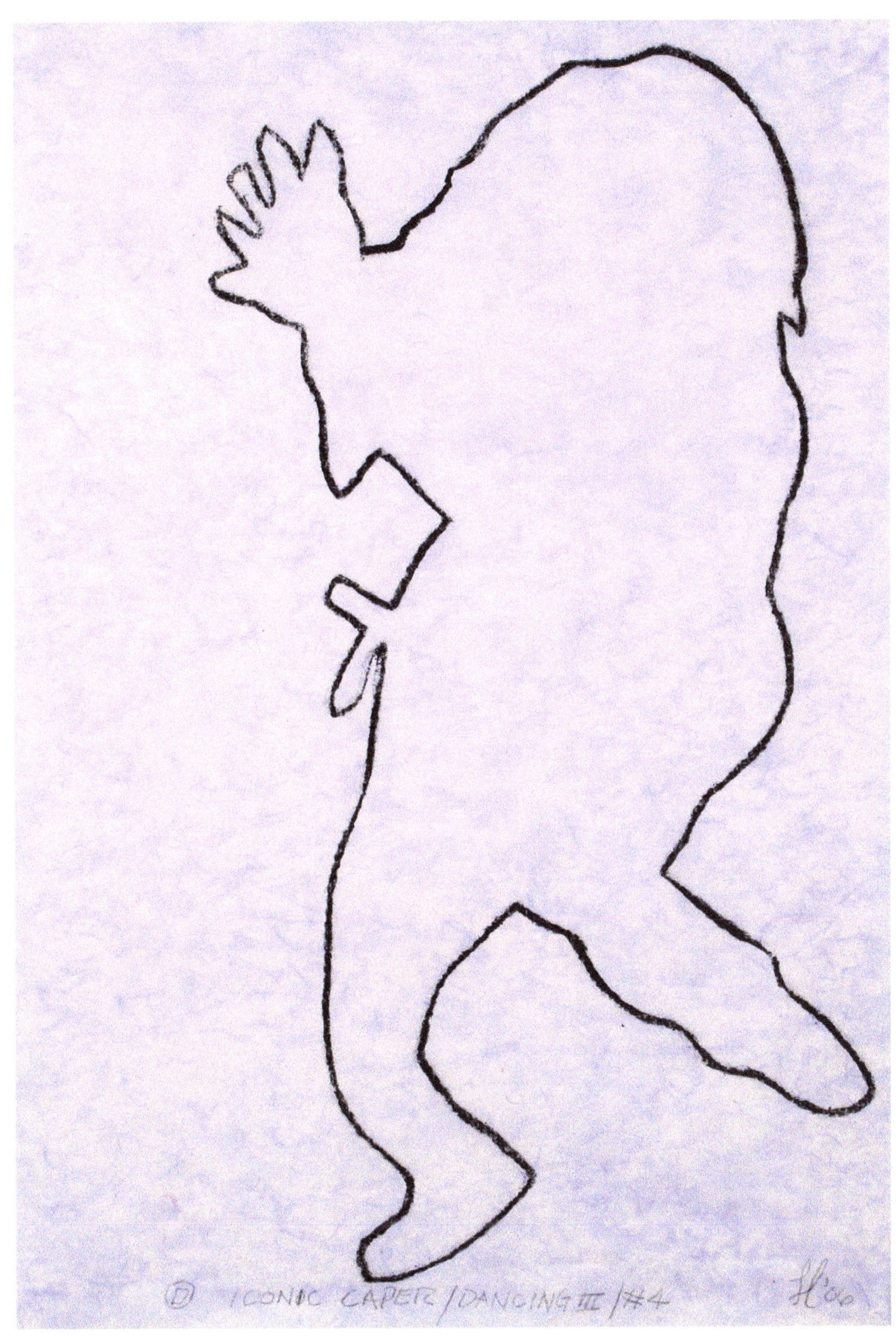

D Iconic Caper / Dancing III, #4, 2006

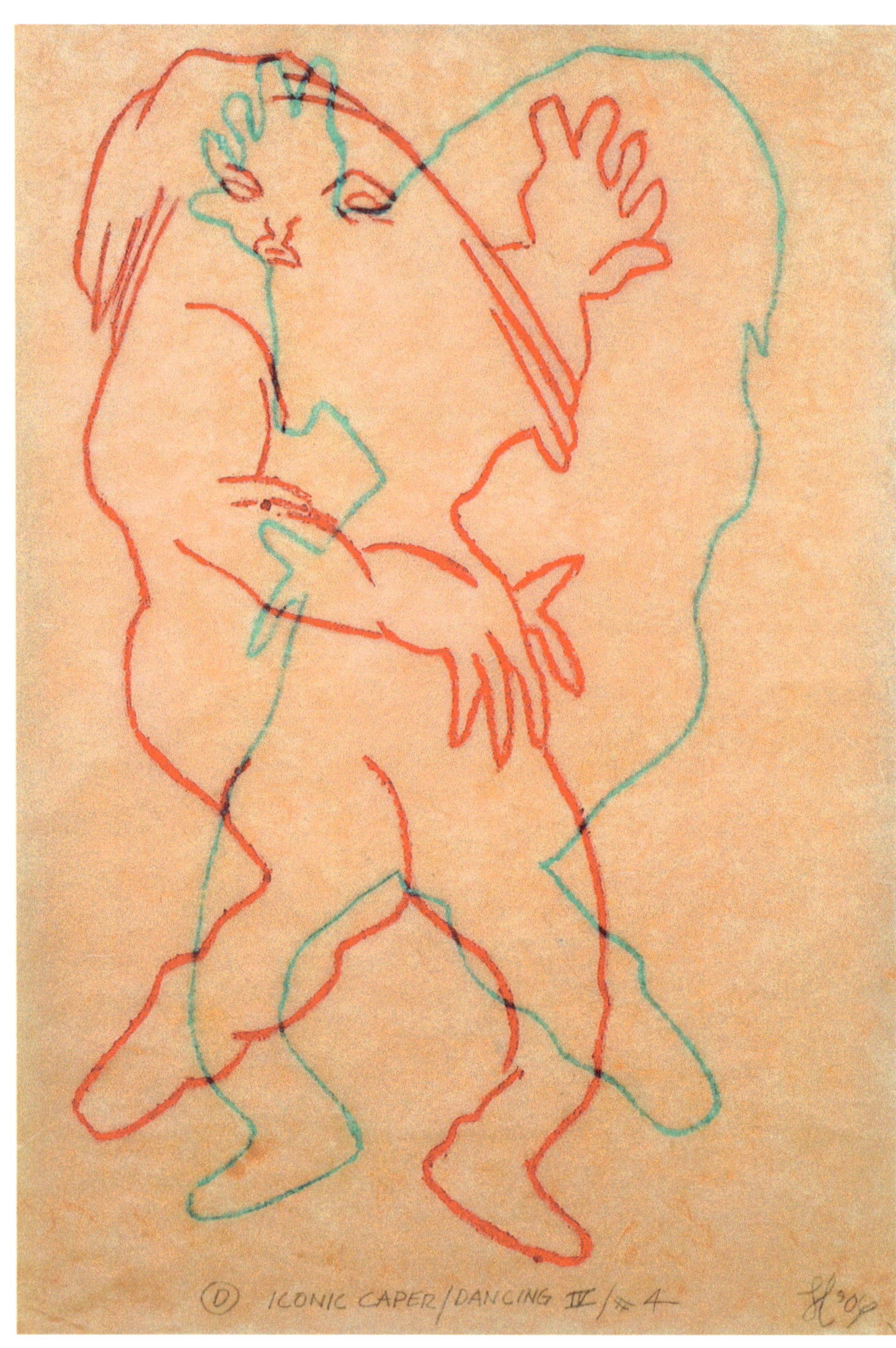

D Iconic Caper / Dancing IV, #4, 2006

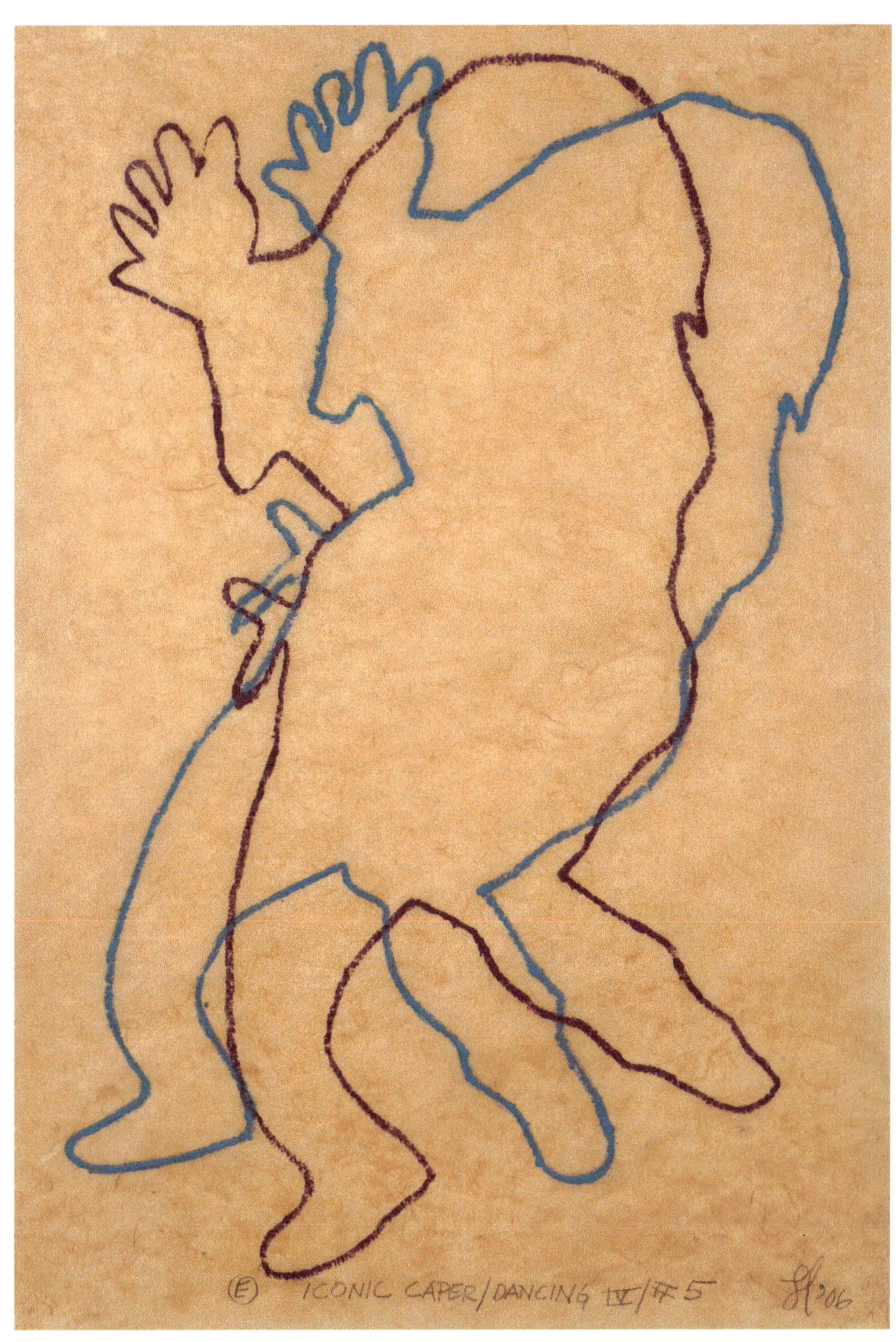

E Iconic Caper / Dancing IV, #5, 2006

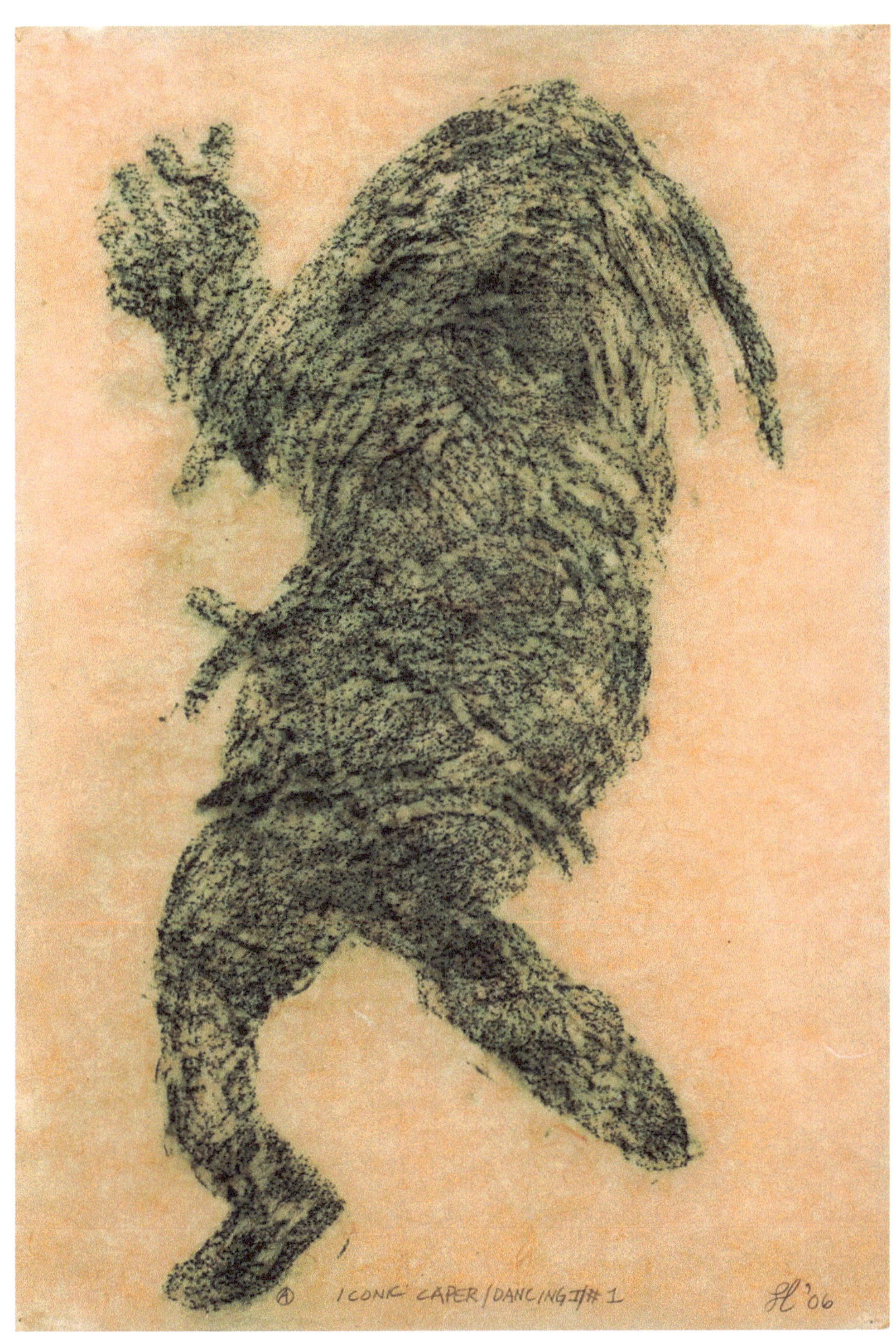

A Iconic Caper / Dancing I, #1, 2006

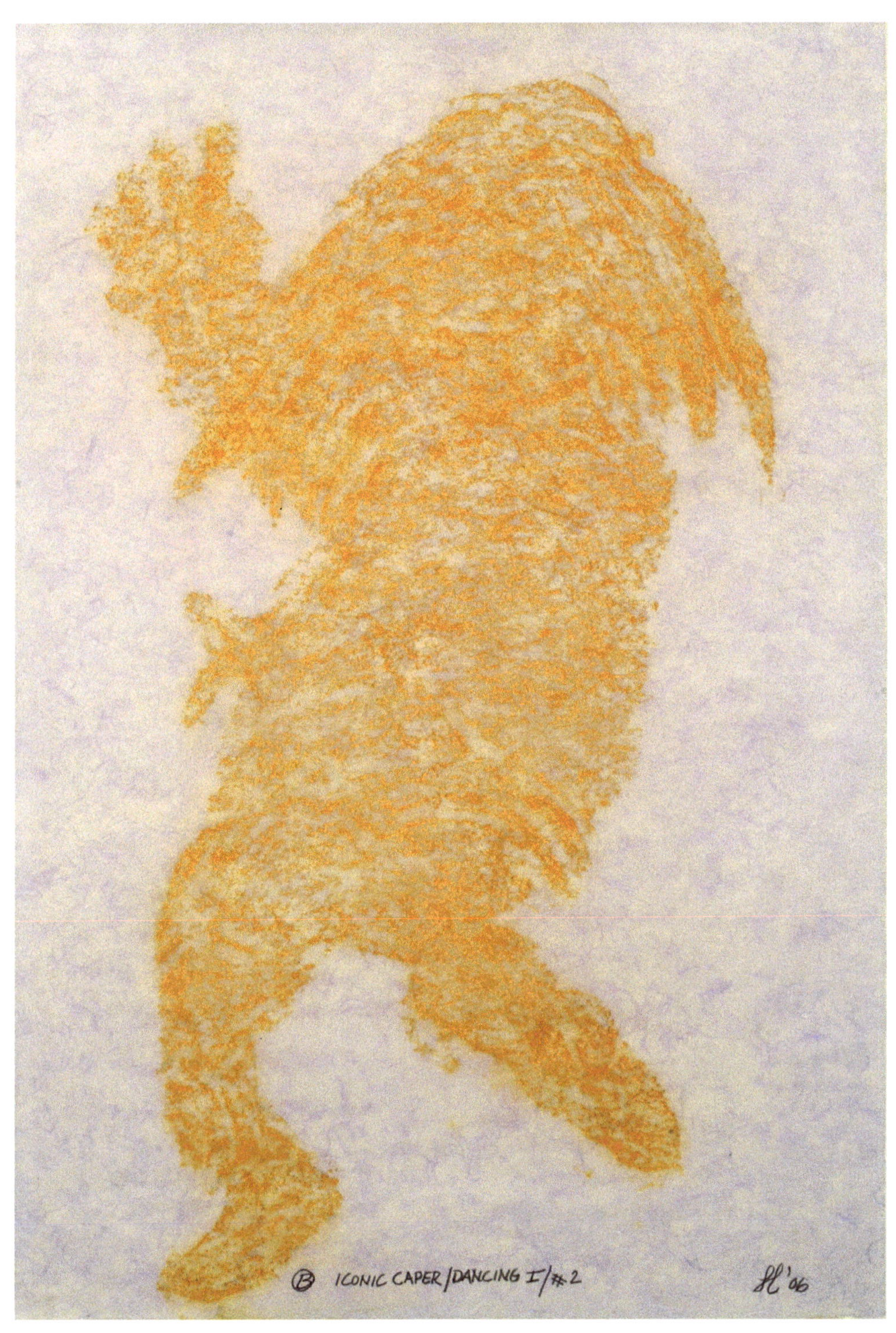

B Iconic Caper / Dancing I, #2, 2006

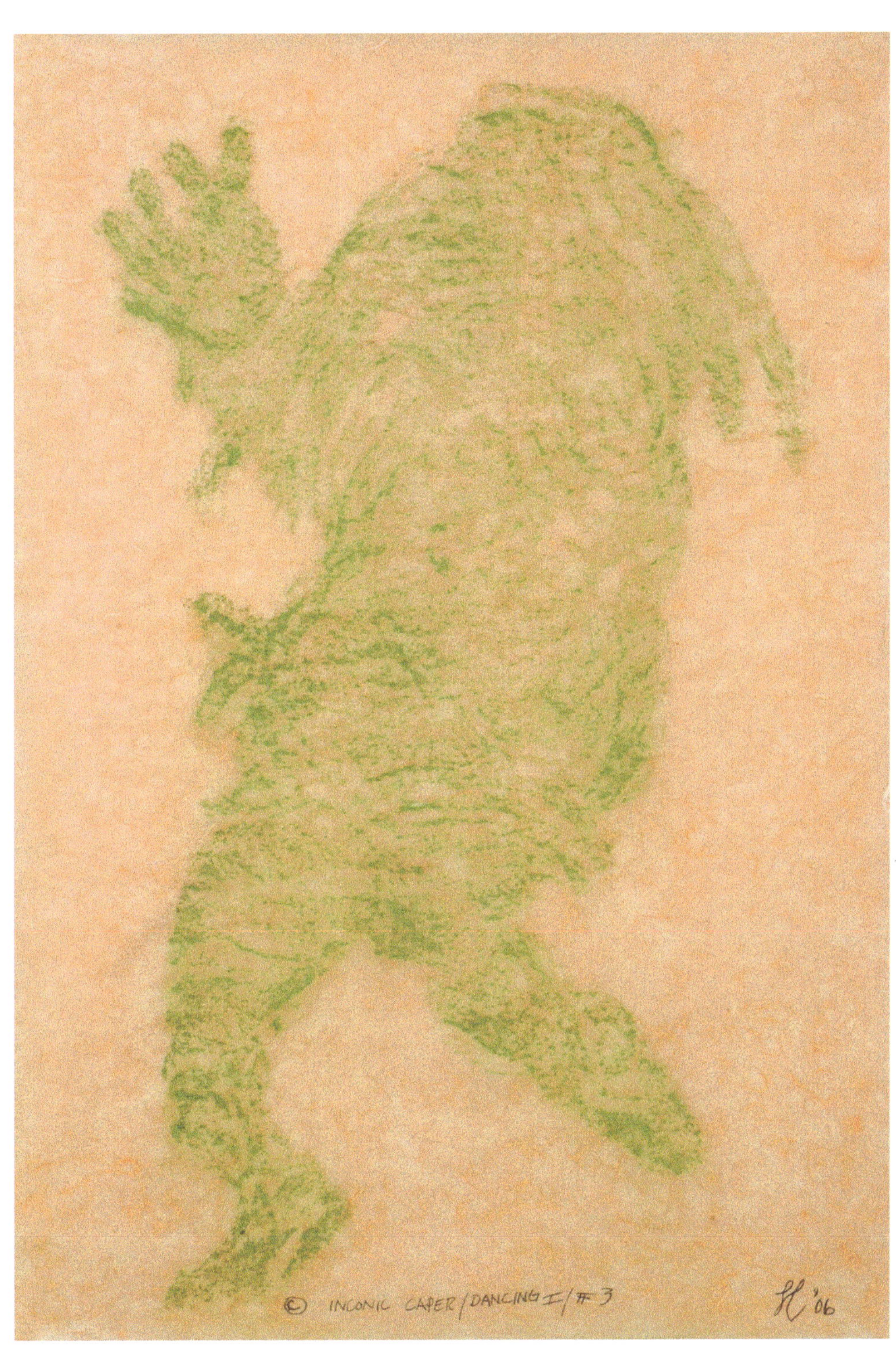

C Iconic Caper / Dancing I, #3, 2006

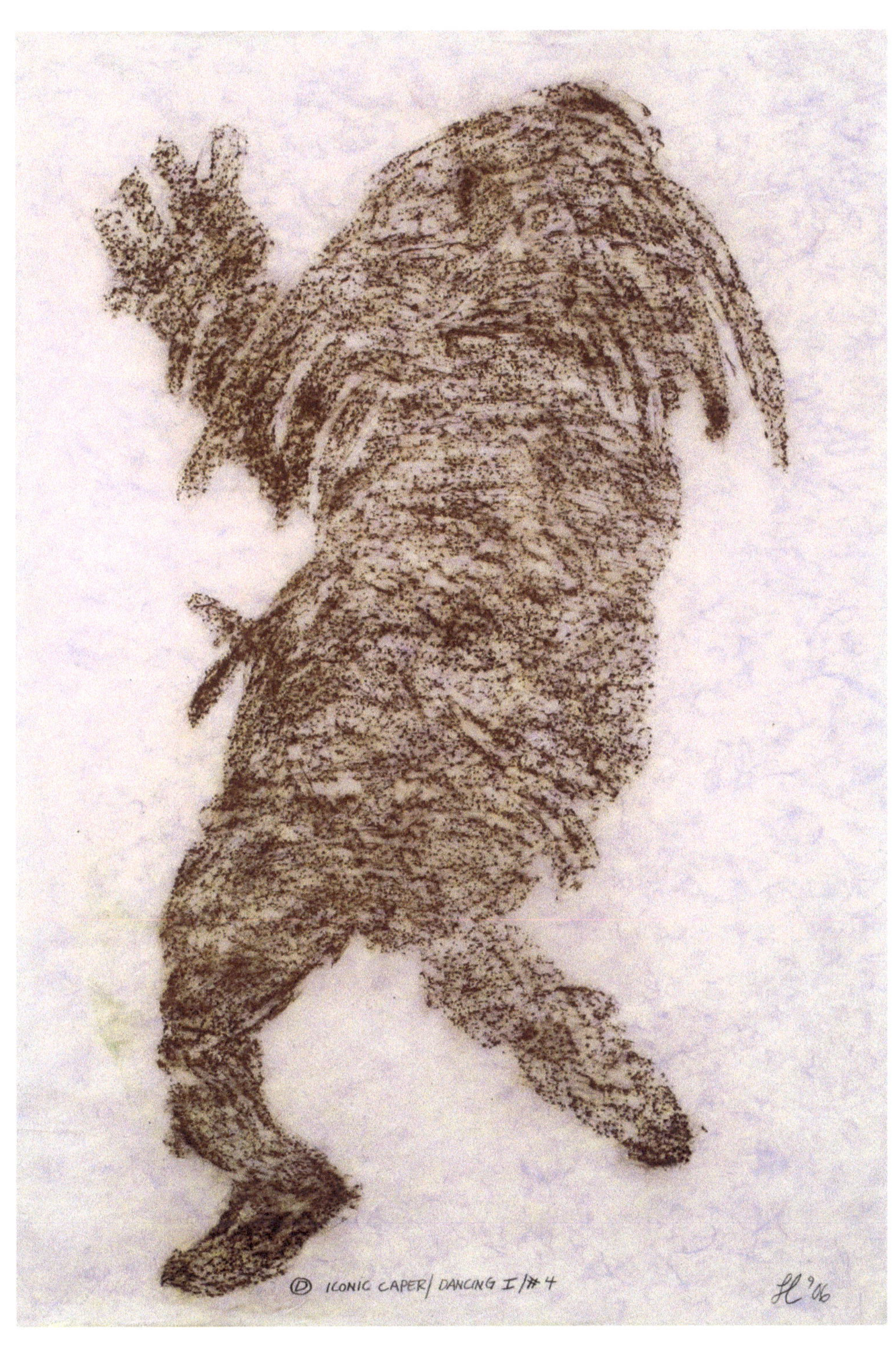

D Iconic Caper / Dancing 1, #4, 2006

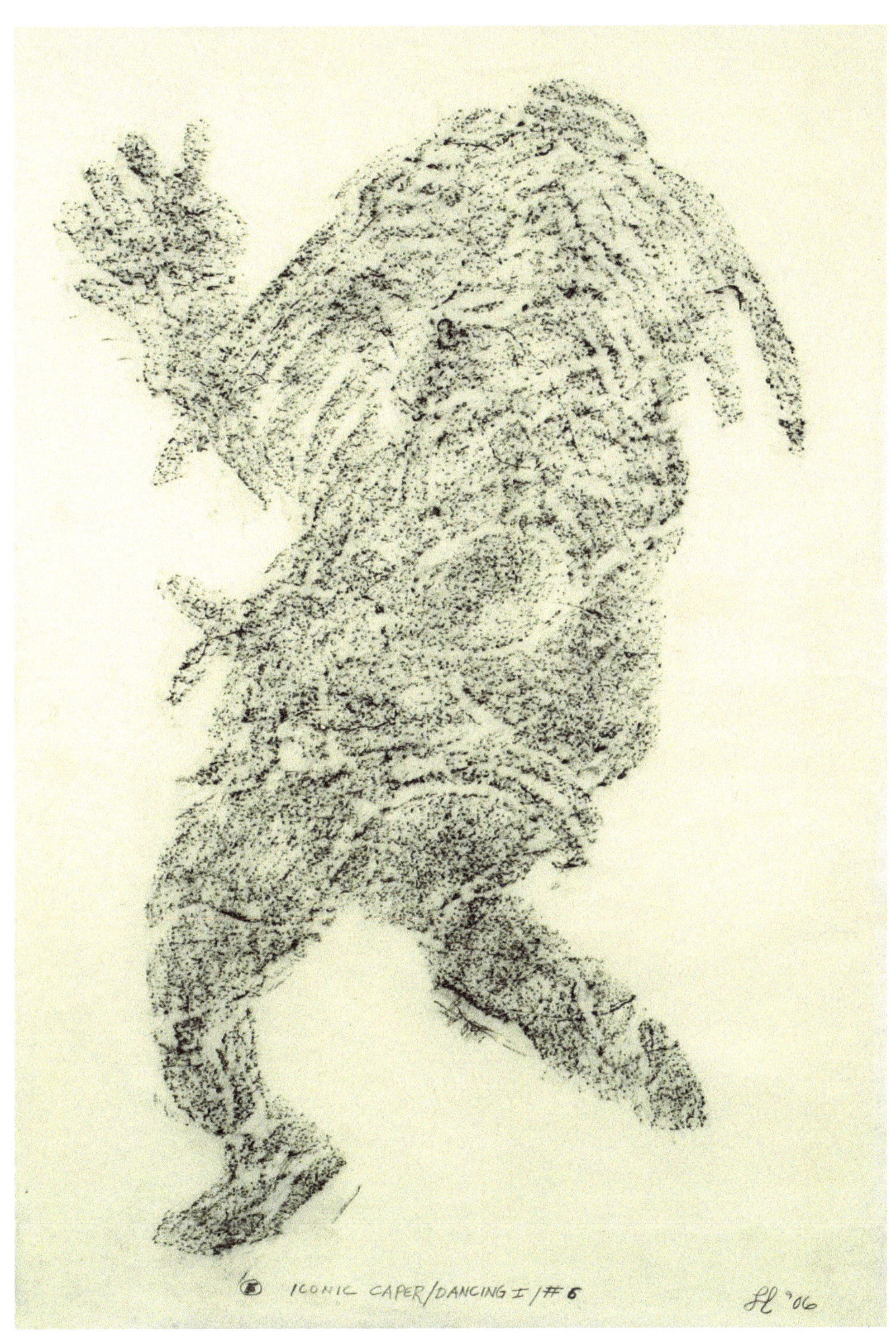

F Iconic Caper / Dancing I, #6, 2006

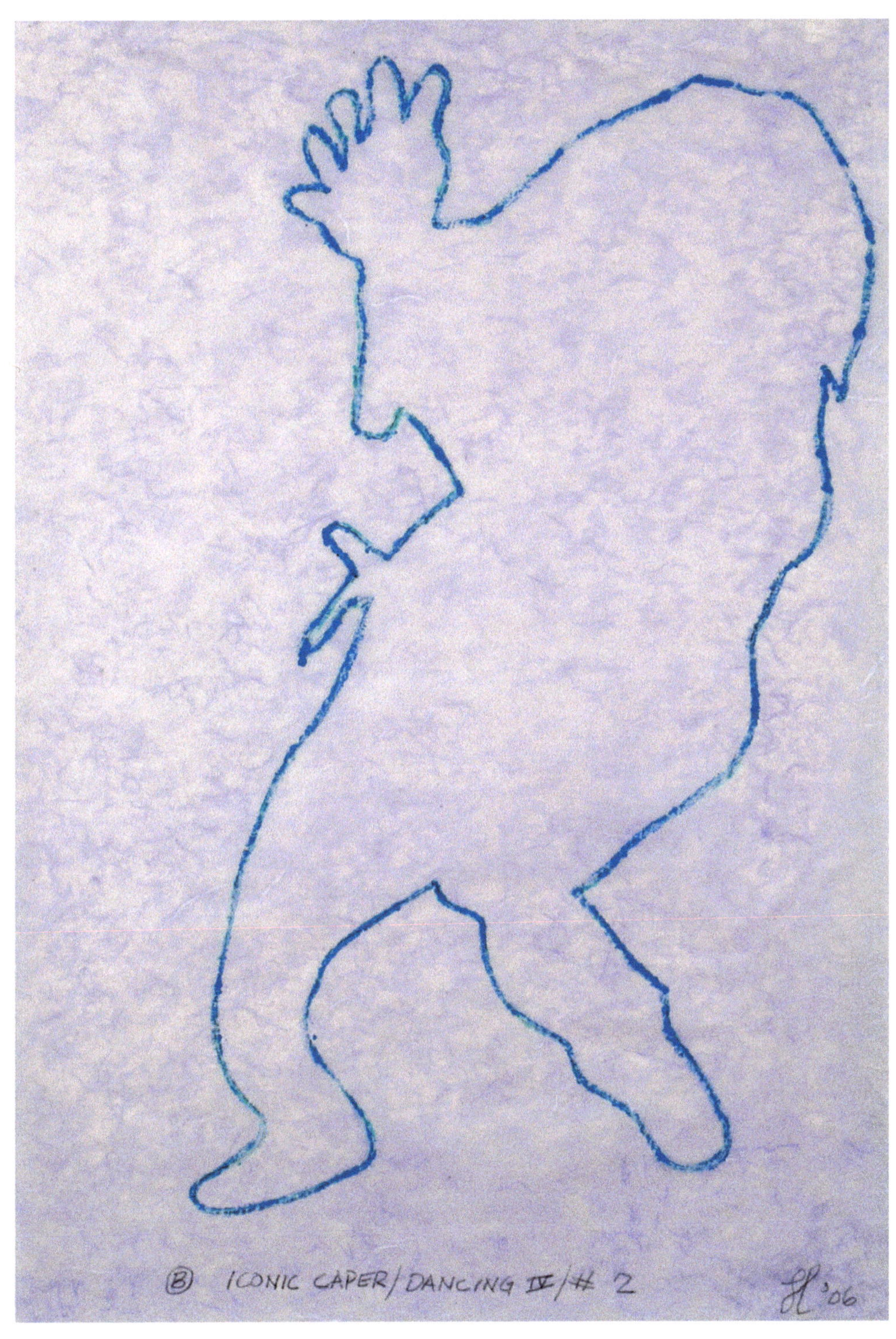

B Iconic Caper / Dancing IV, #2, 2006

The Hip-Hop Allegories

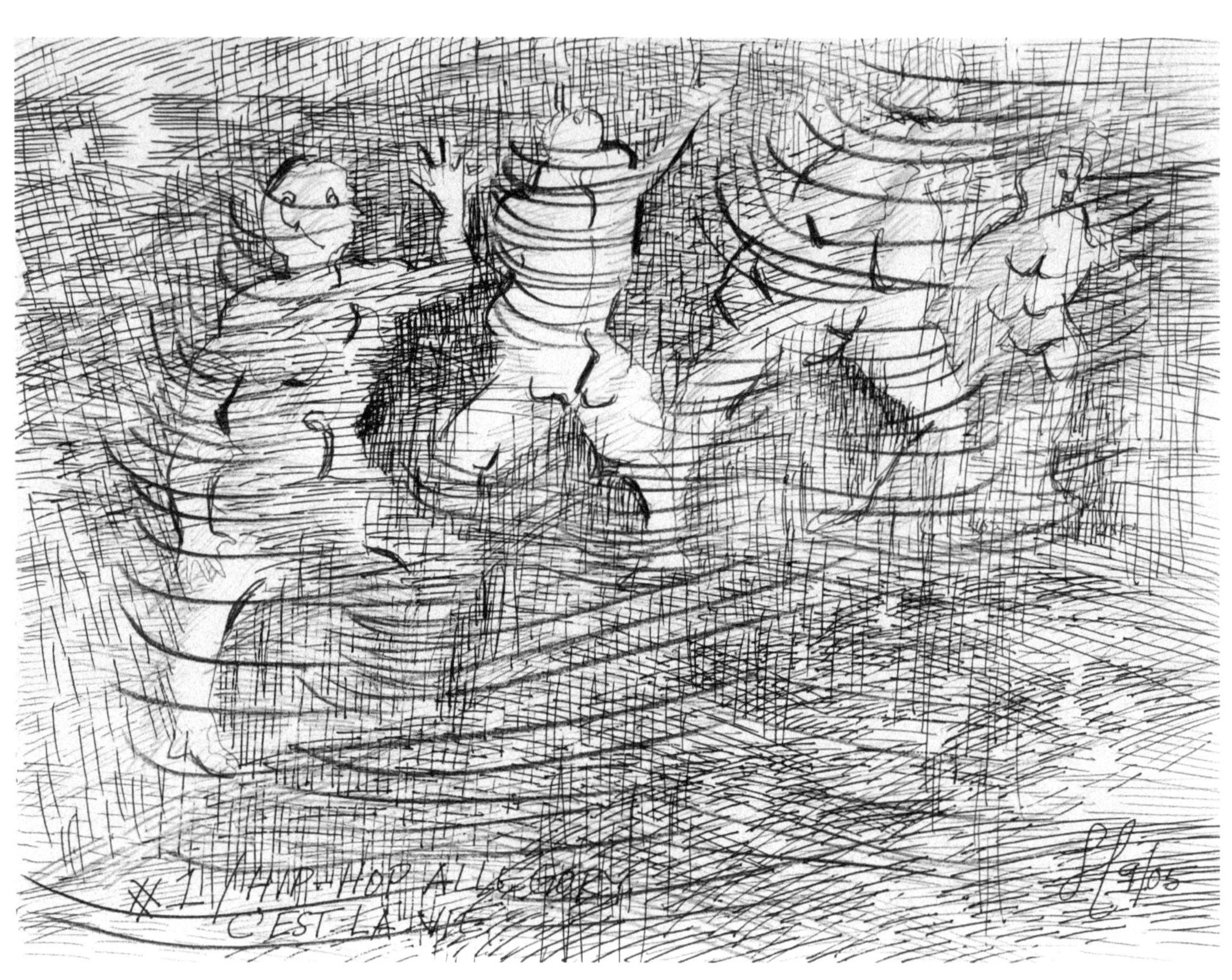

Hip-Hop Allegory ~ C'est La Vie #1, 2005

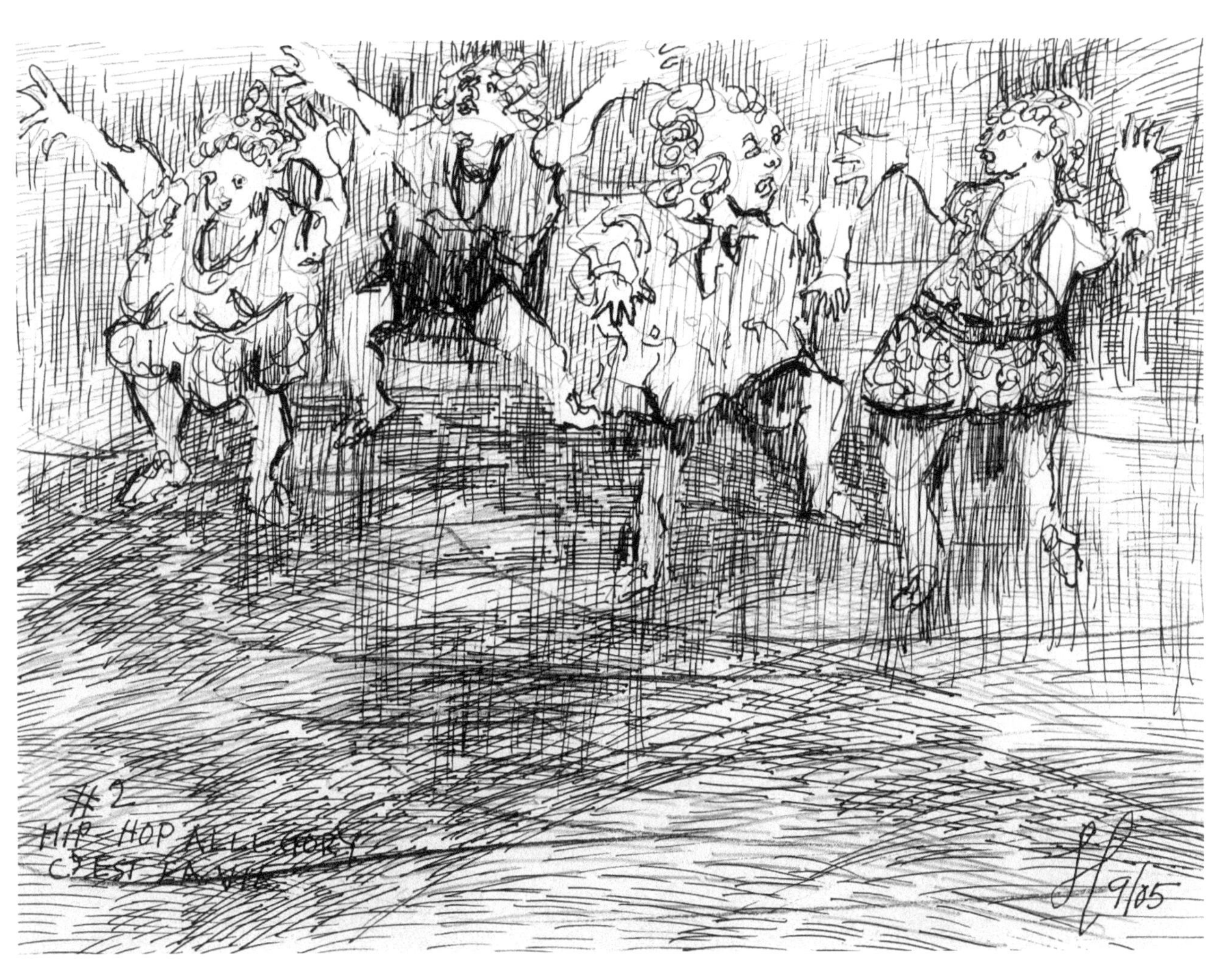

Hip-Hop Allegory ~ C'est La Vie #2, 2005

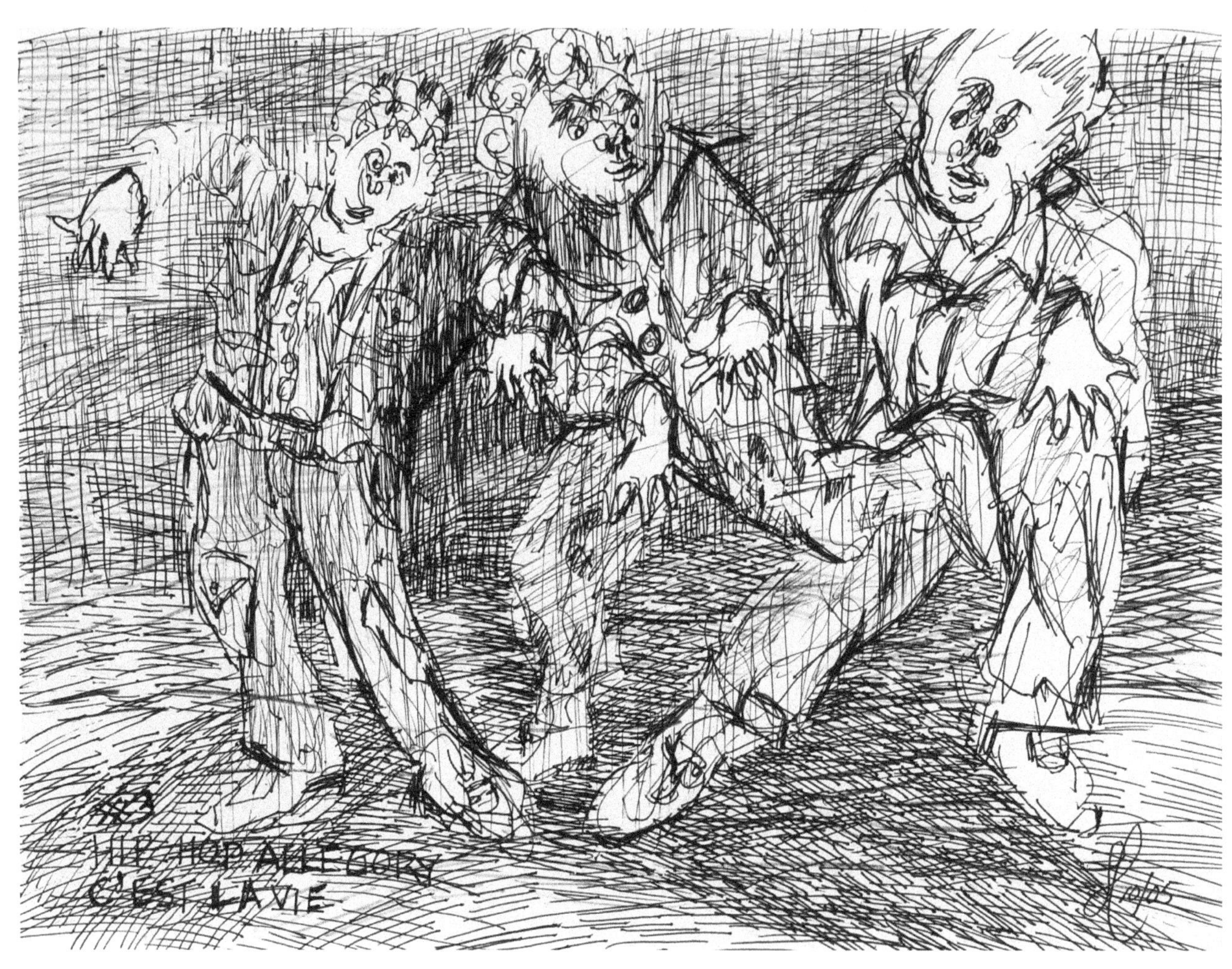

Hip-Hop Allegory ~ C'est La Vie #3, 2005

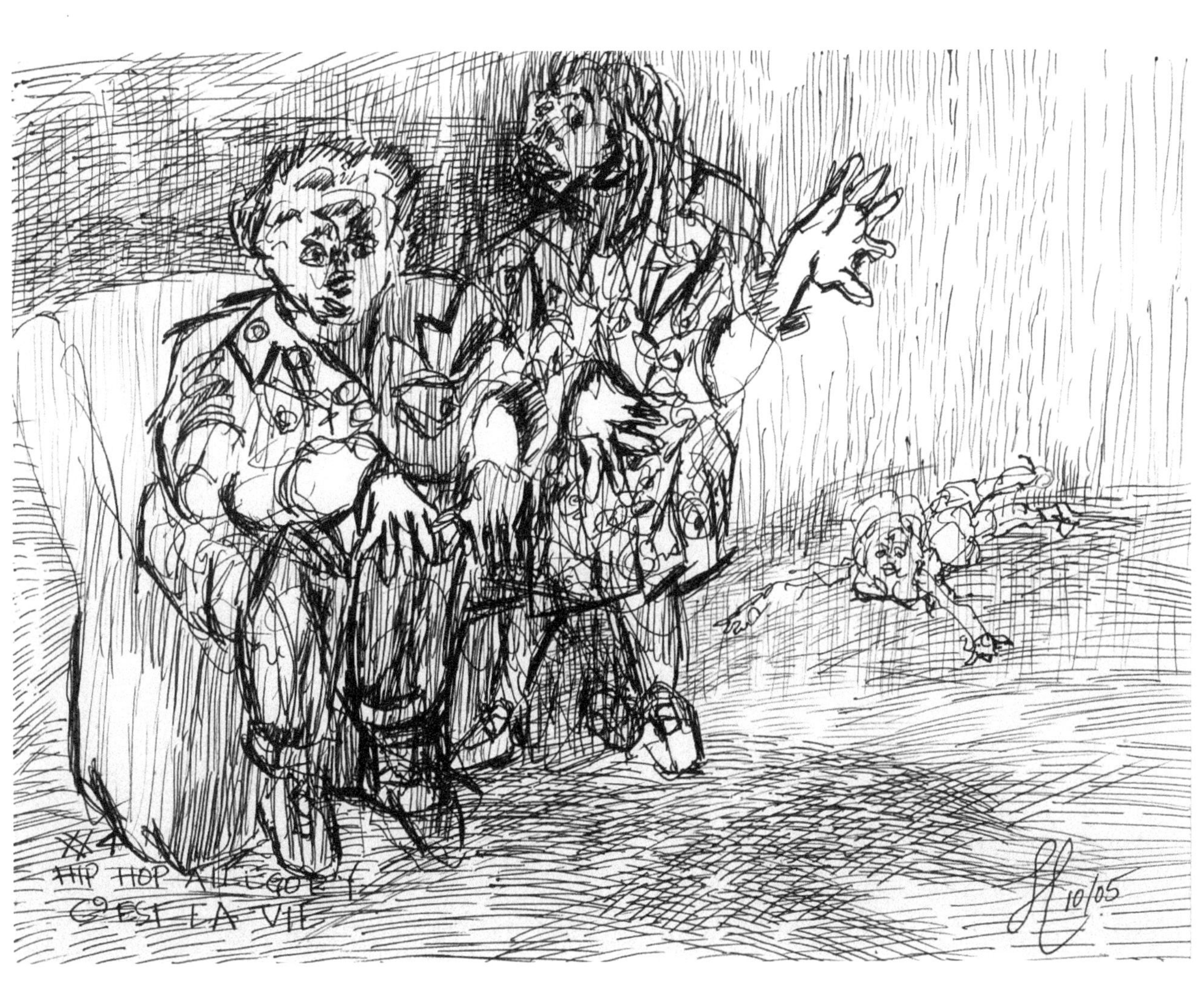

Hip-Hop Allegory ~ C'est La Vie #4, 2005

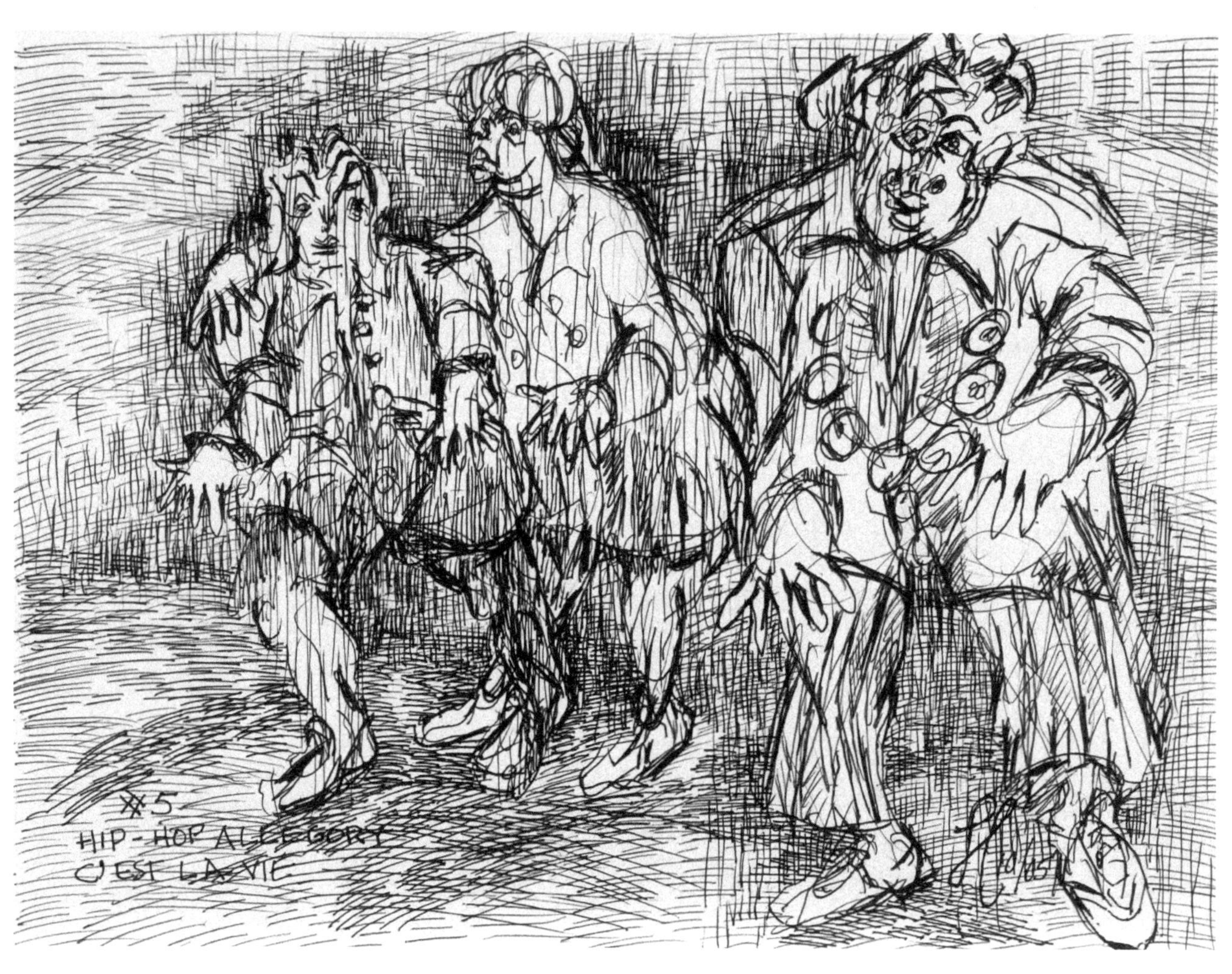

Hip-Hop Allegory ~ C'est La Vie #5, 2005

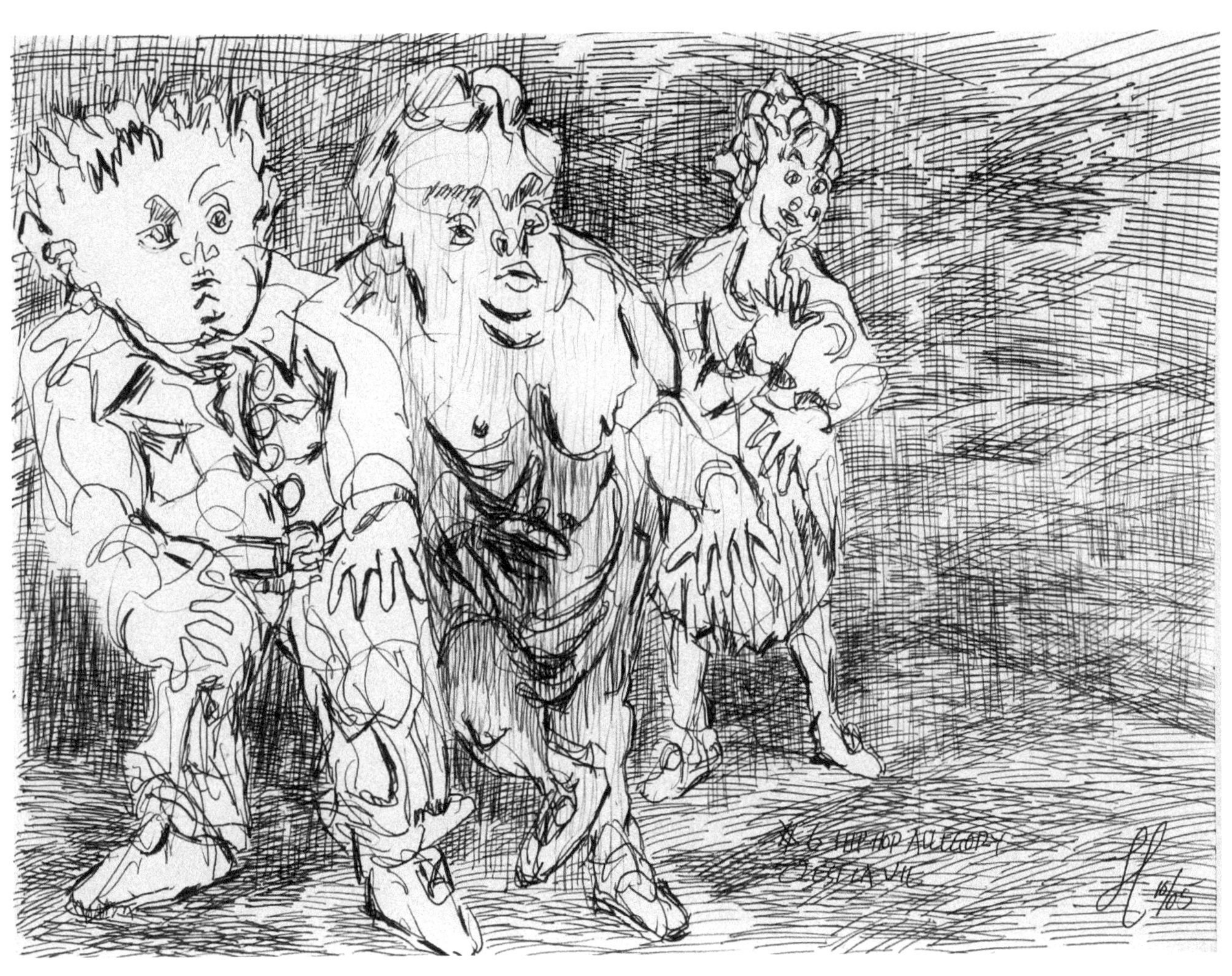

Hip-Hop Allegory ~ C'est La Vie #6, 2005

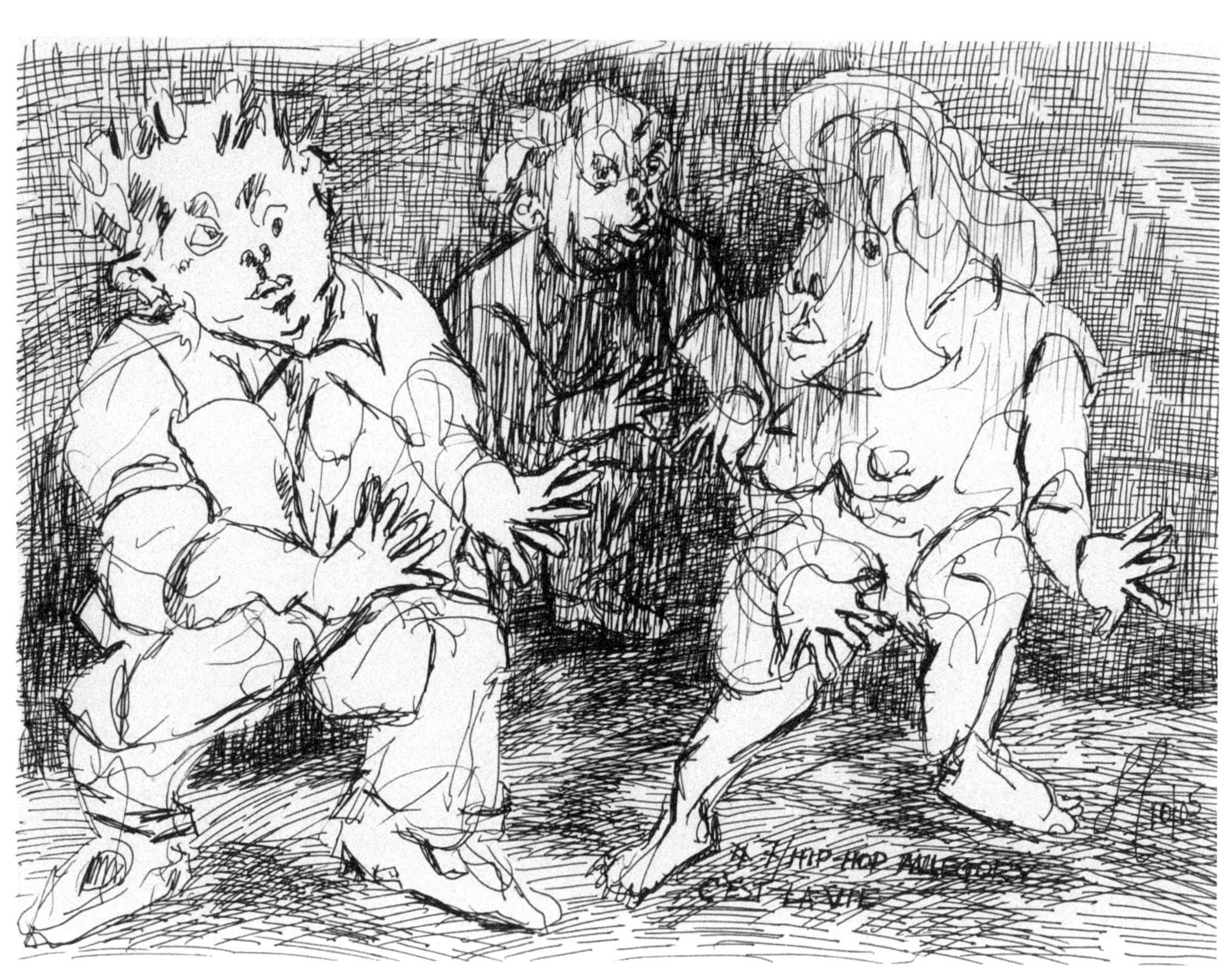

Hip-Hop Allegory ~ C'est La Vie #7, 2005

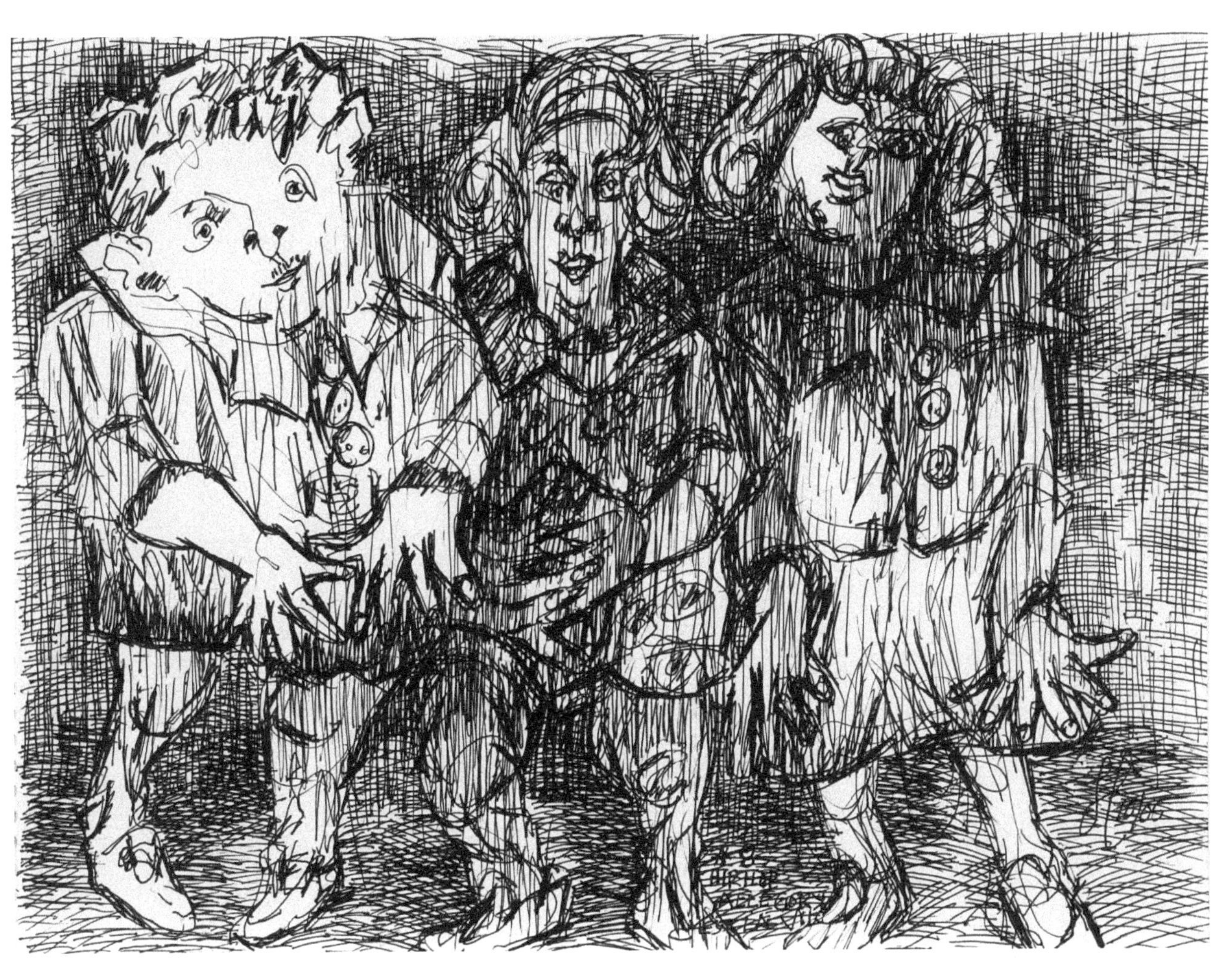

Hip-Hop Allegory ~ C'est La Vie #8, 2005

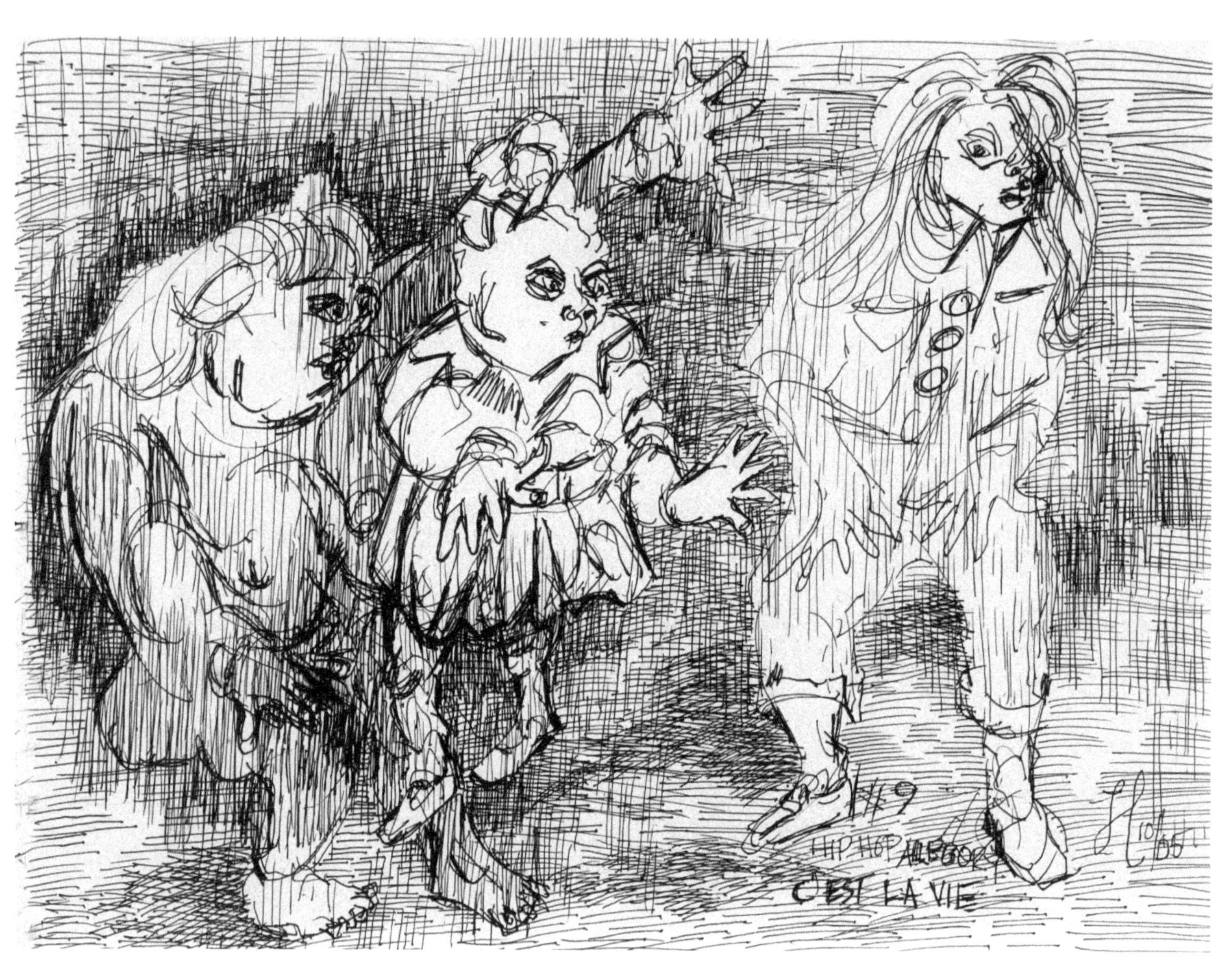

Hip-Hop Allegory ~ C'est La Vie #9, 2005

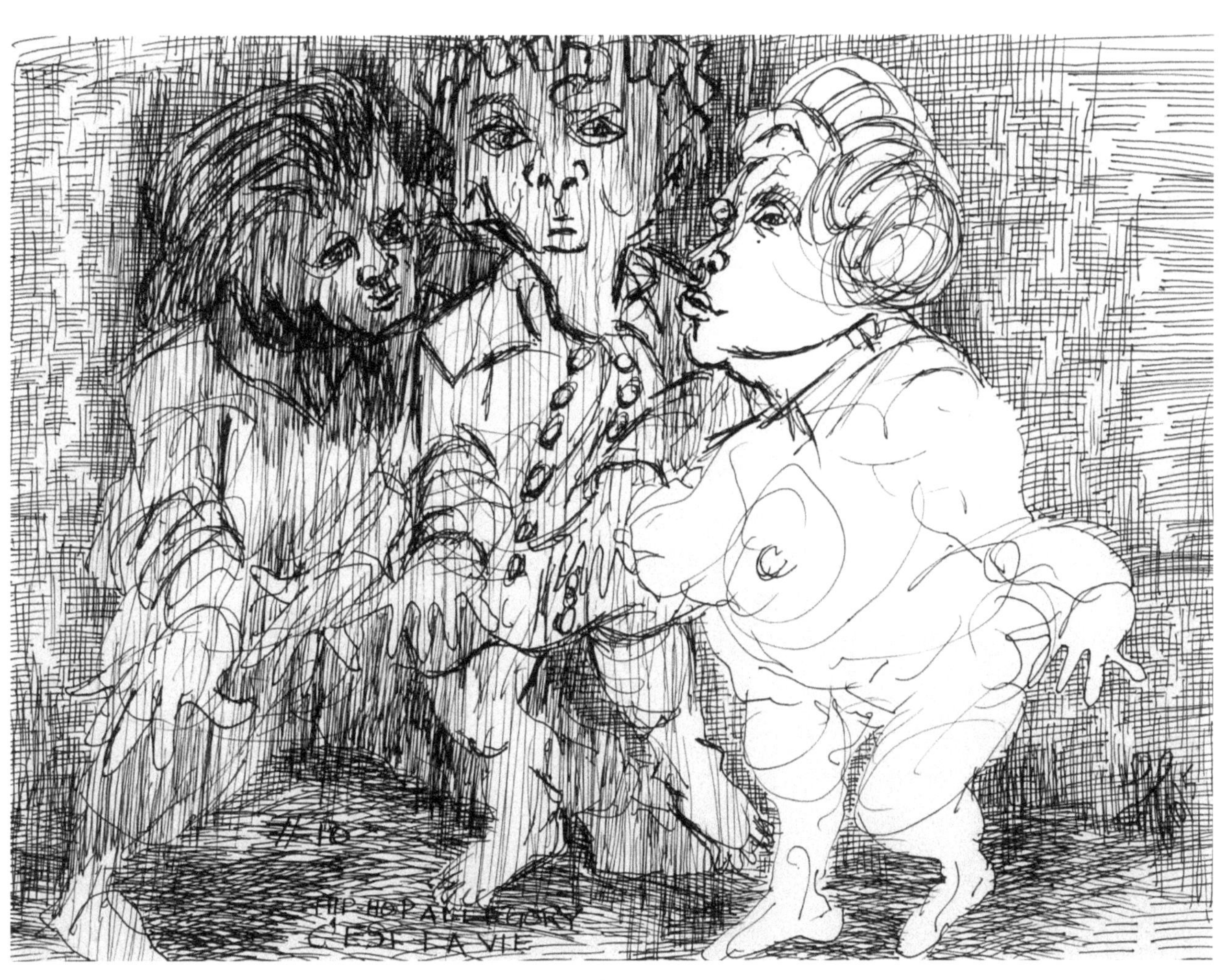

Hip-Hop Allegory ~ C'est La Vie #10, 2005

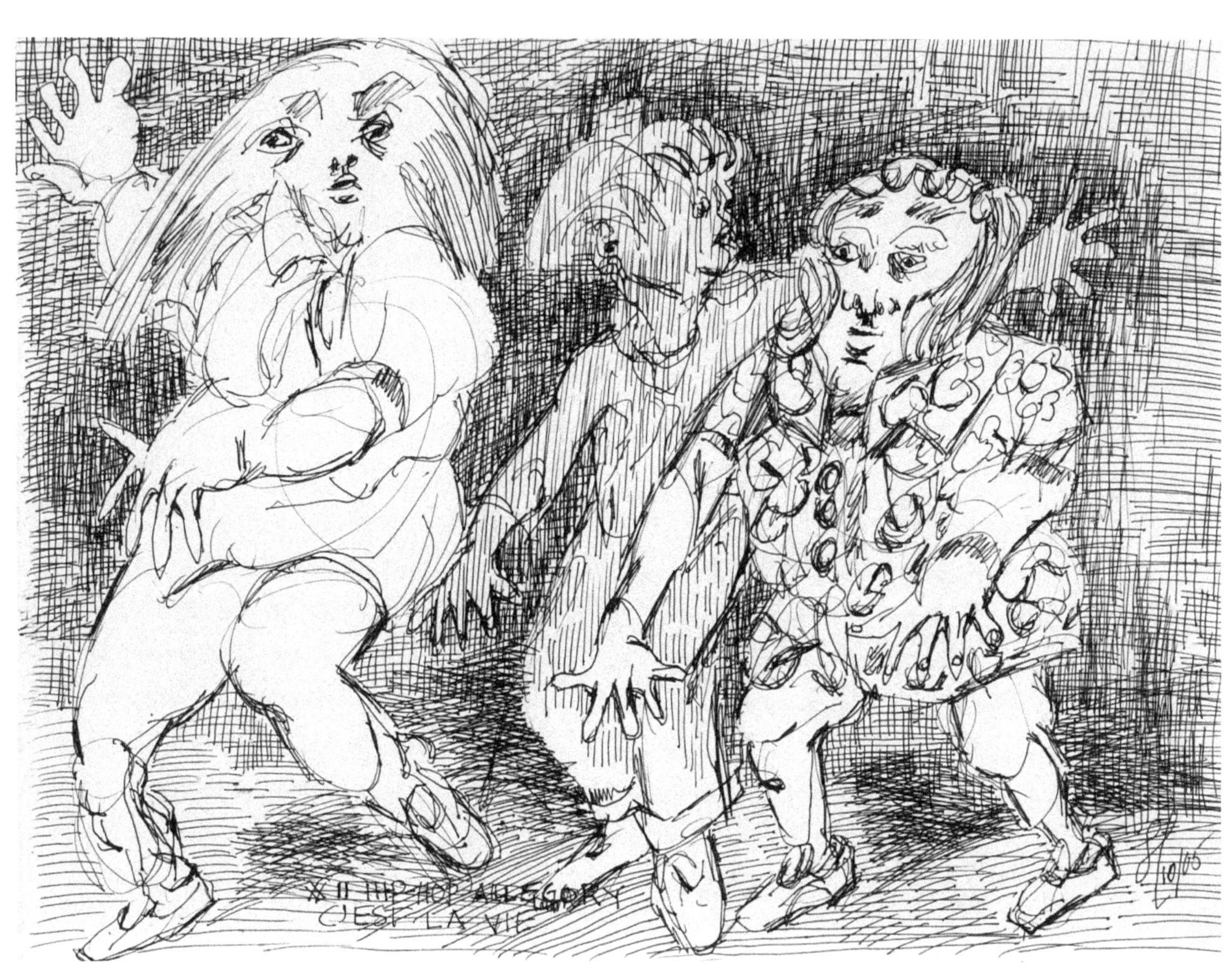

Hip-Hop Allegory ~ C'est La Vie #11, 2005

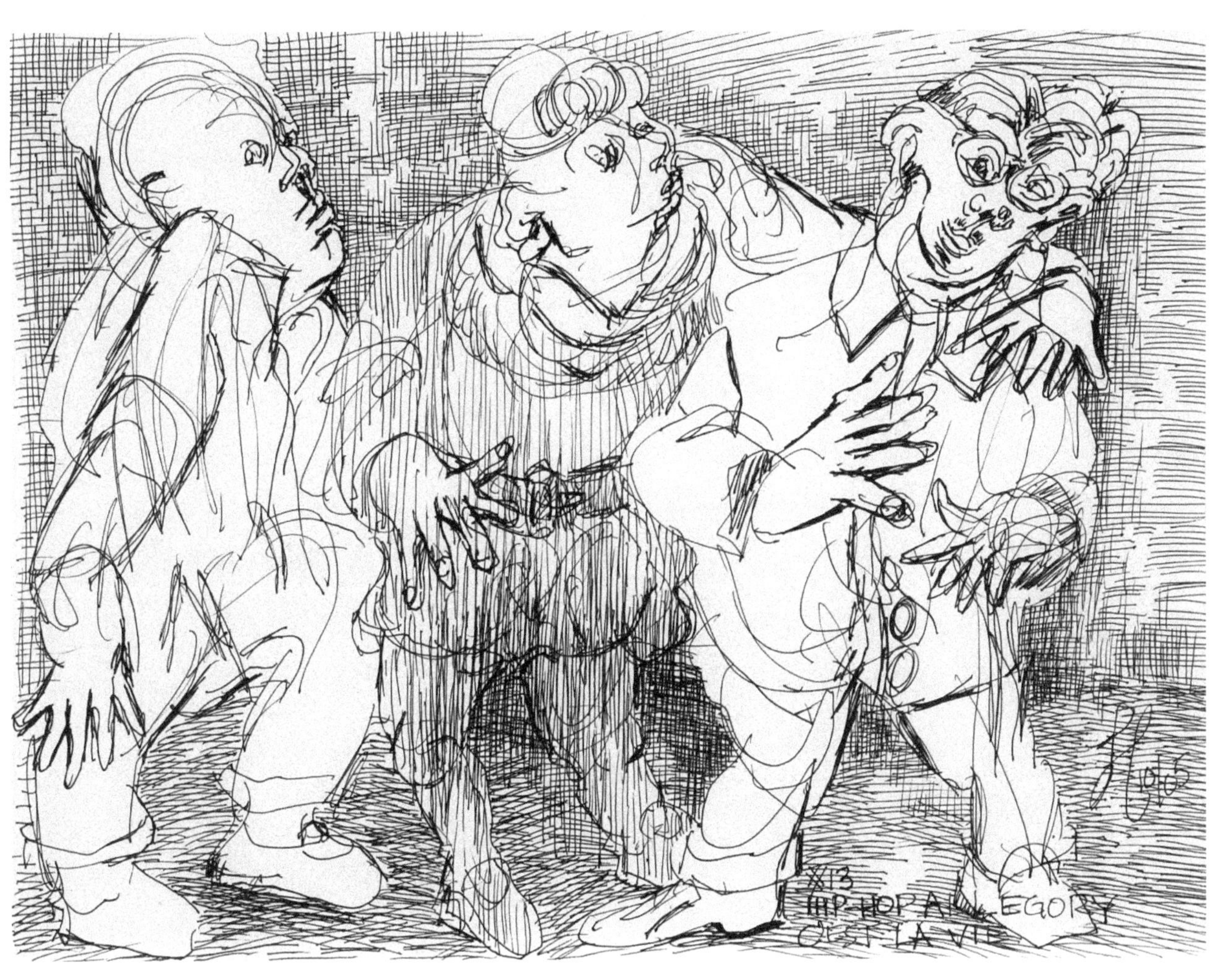

Hip-Hop Allegory ~ C'est La Vie #13, 2006

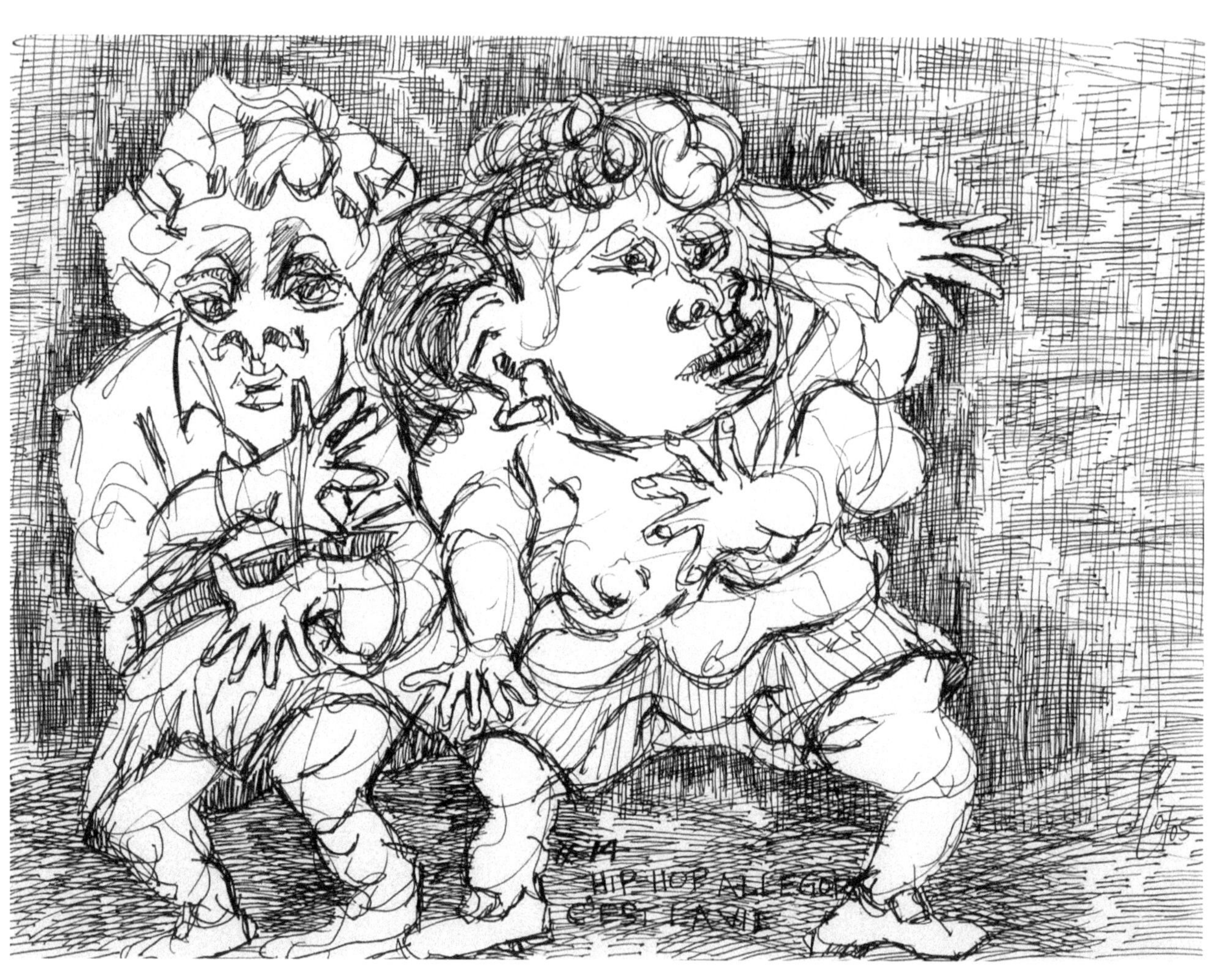

Hip-Hop Allegory ~ C'est La Vie #14, 2005

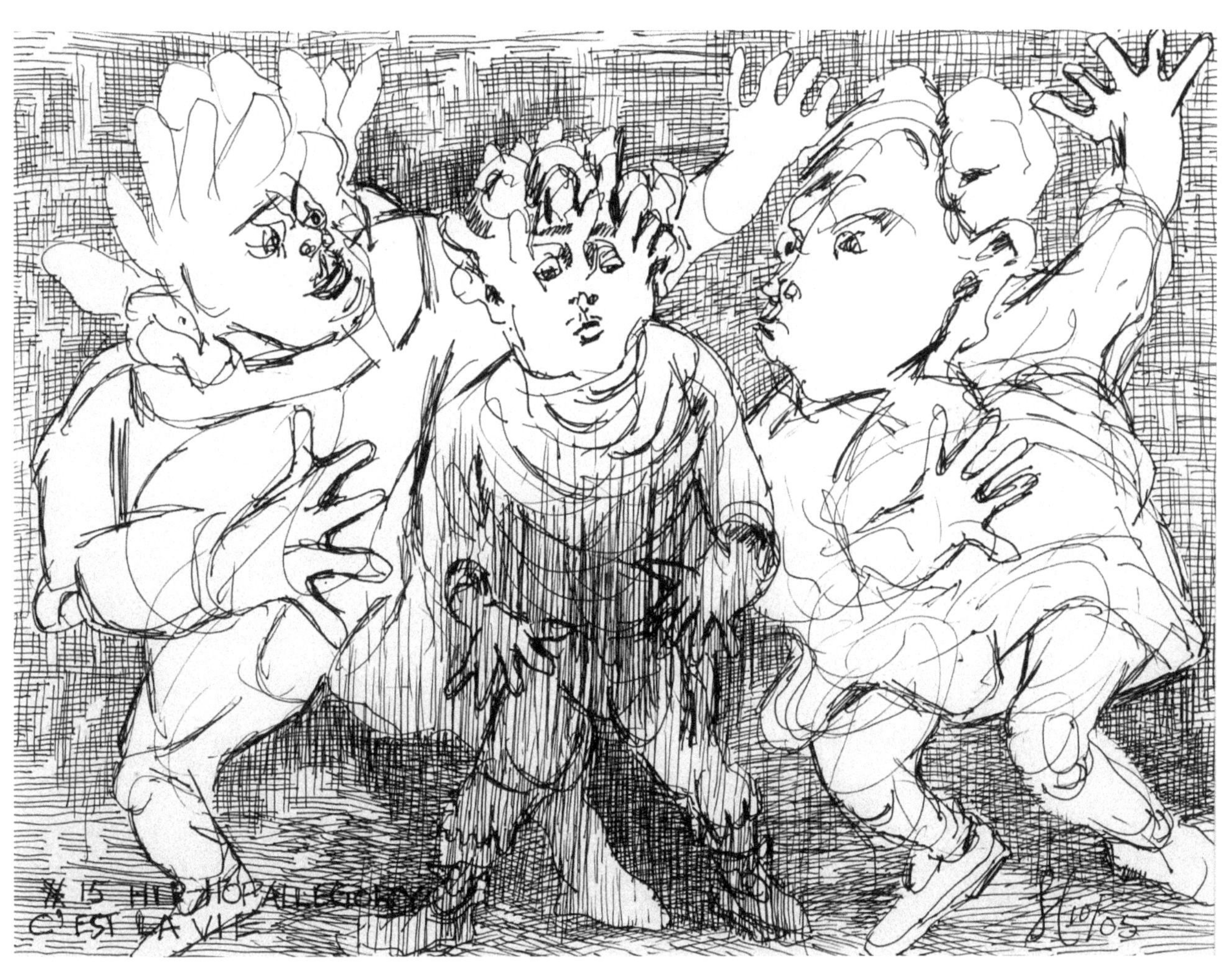

Hip-Hop Allegory ~ C'est La Vie #15, 2005

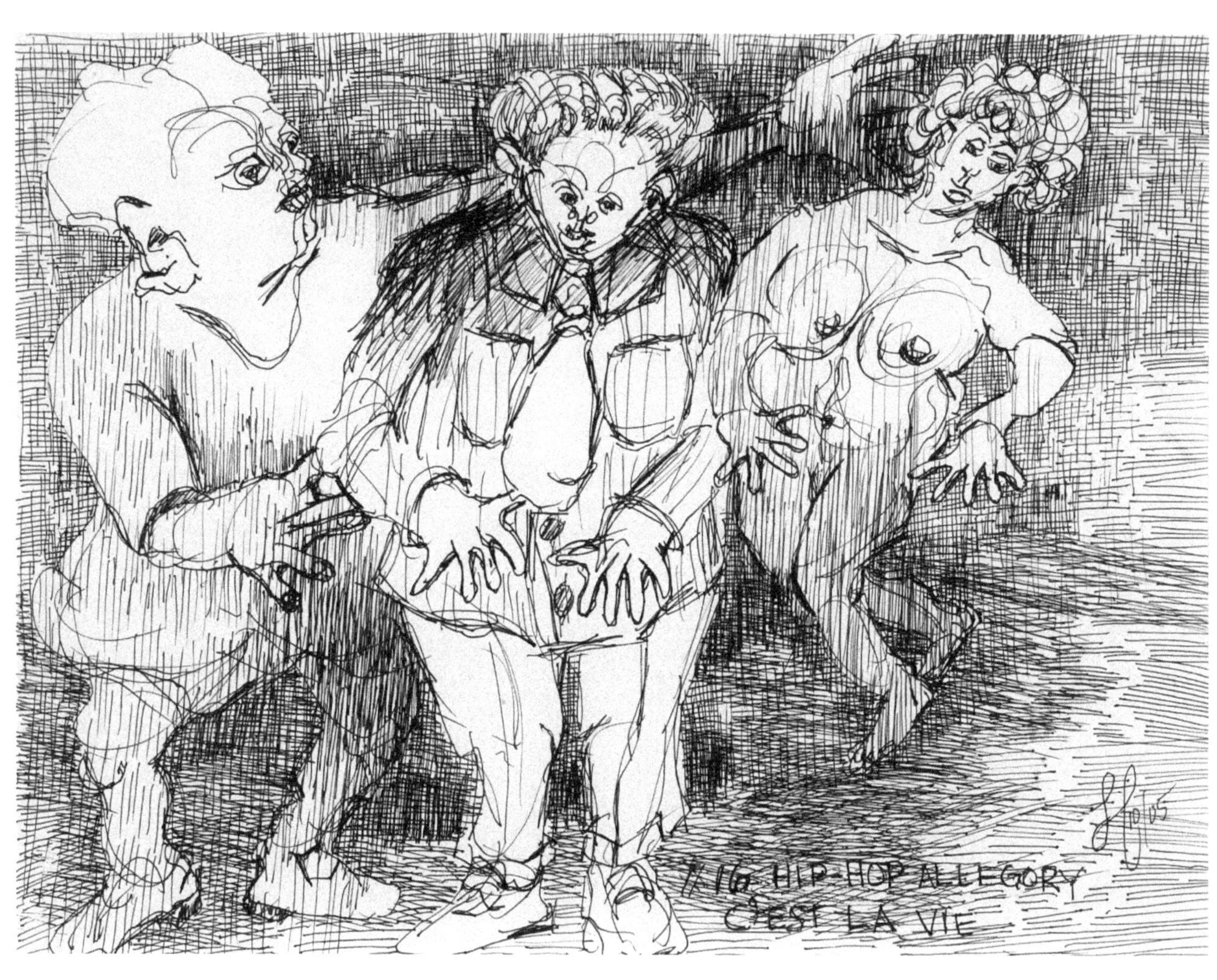

Hip-Hop Allegory ~ C'est La Vie #16, 2005

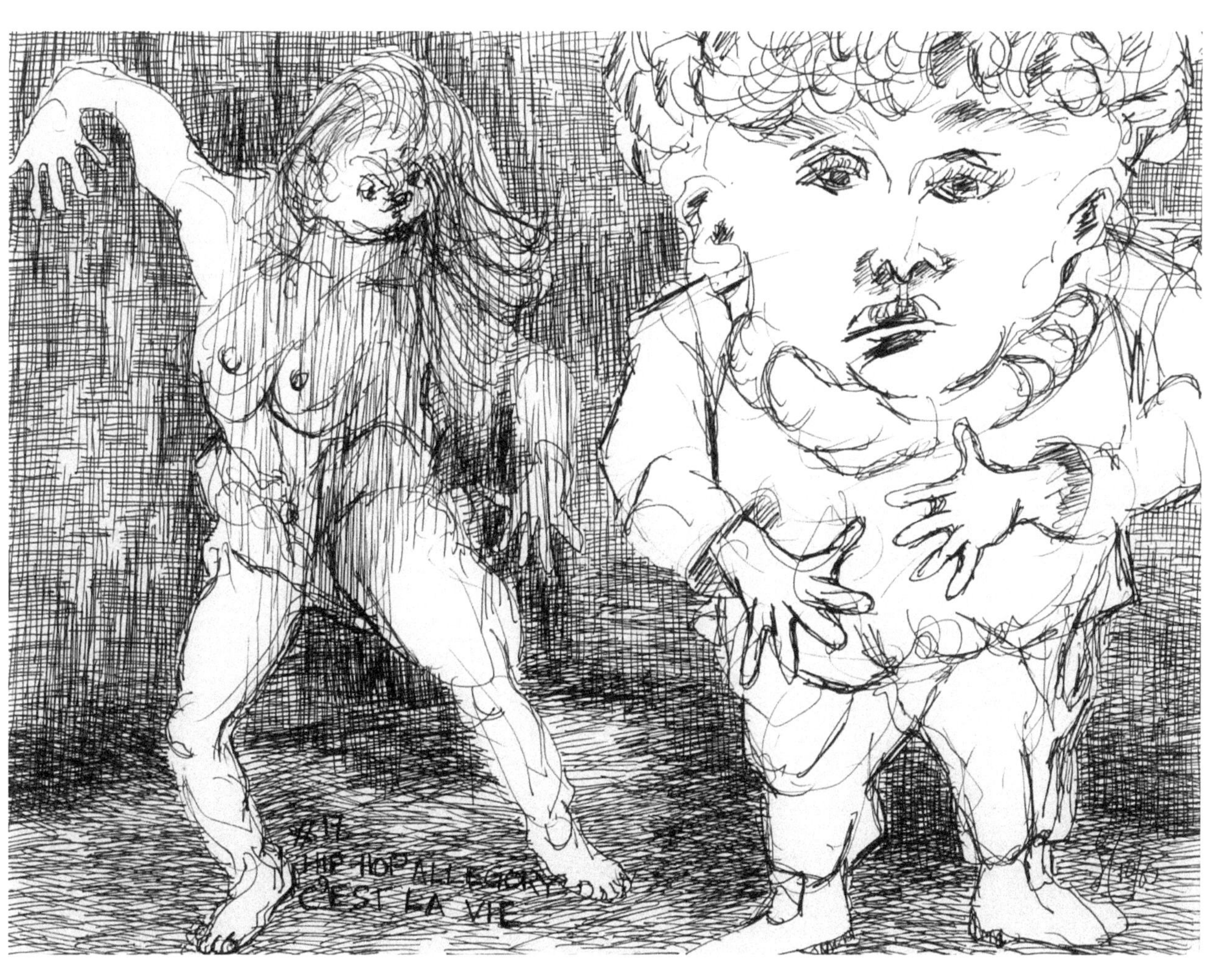

Hip-Hop Allegory ~ C'est La Vie #17, 2005

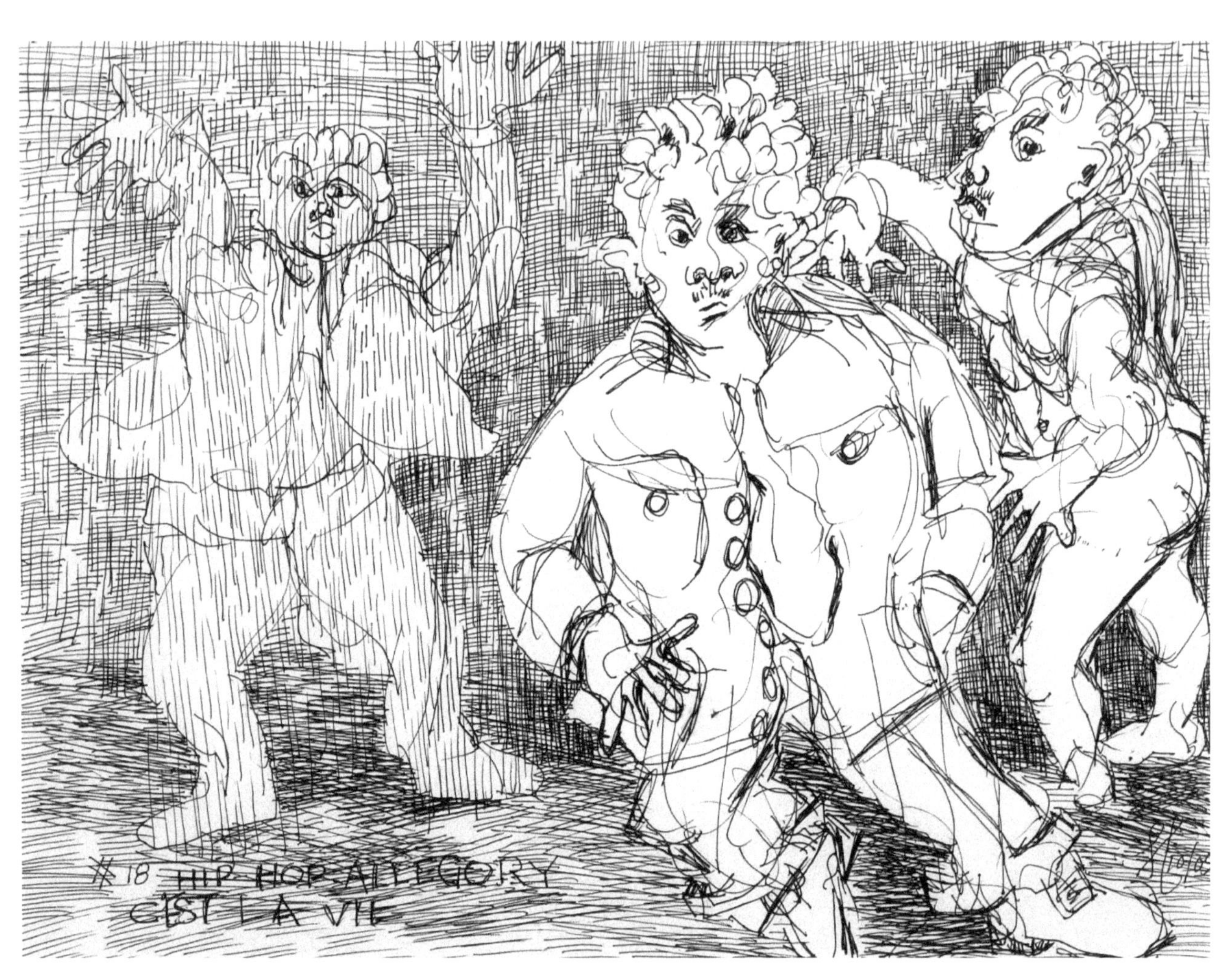

Hip-Hop Allegory ~ C'est La Vie #18, 2005

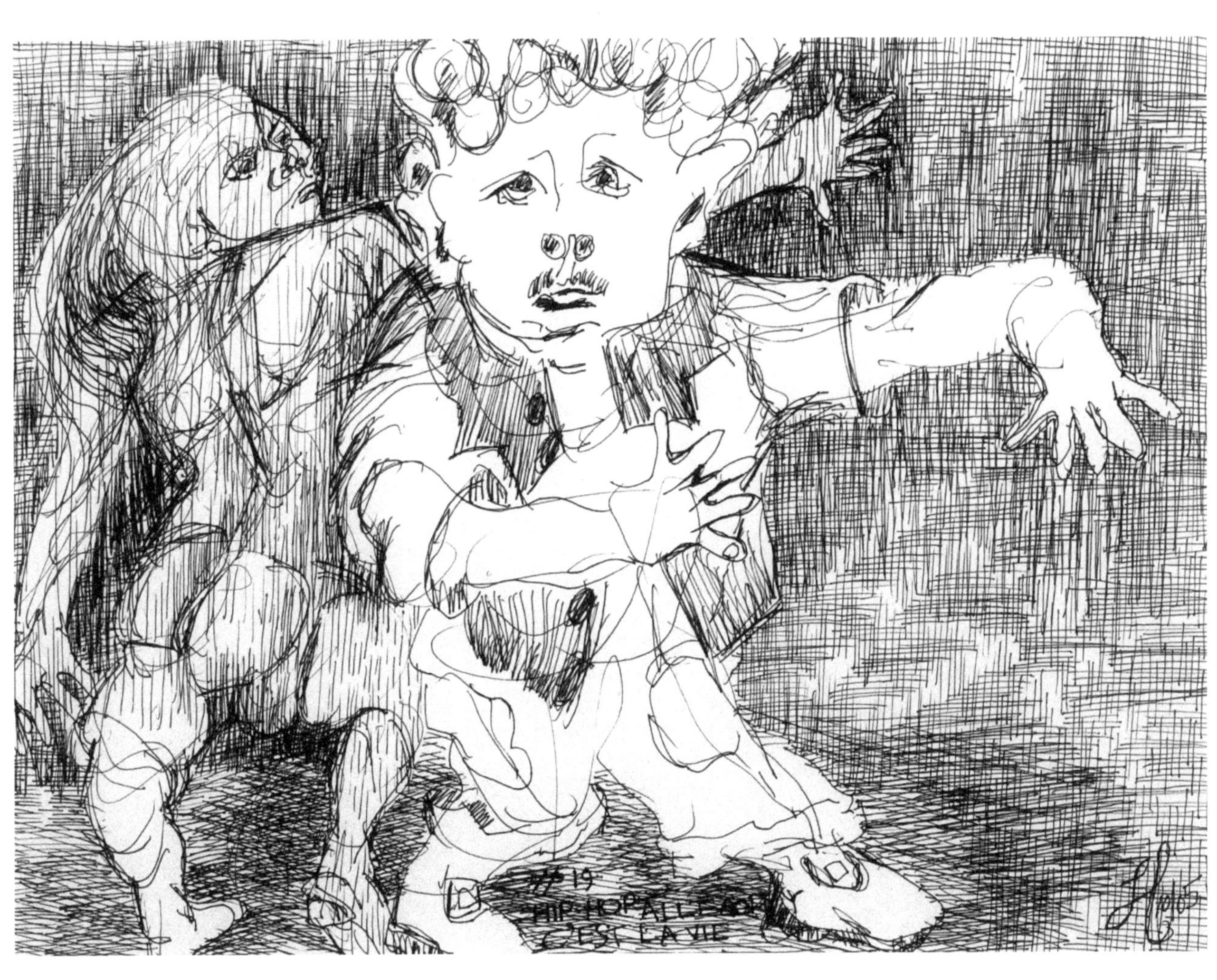

Hip-Hop Allegory ~ C'est La Vie #19, 2005

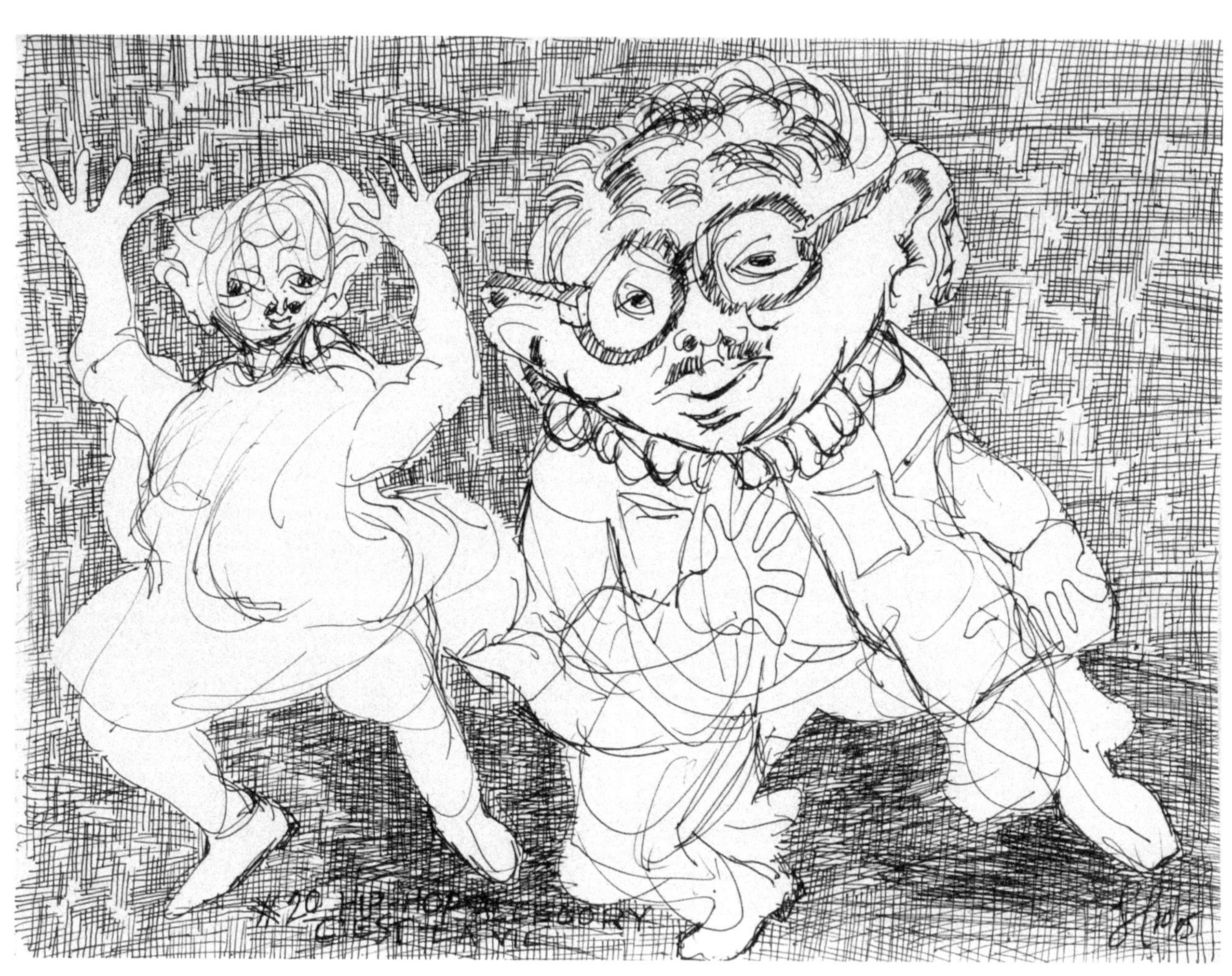

Hip-Hop Allegory ~ C'est La Vie #20, 2005

Three Sinks X Series

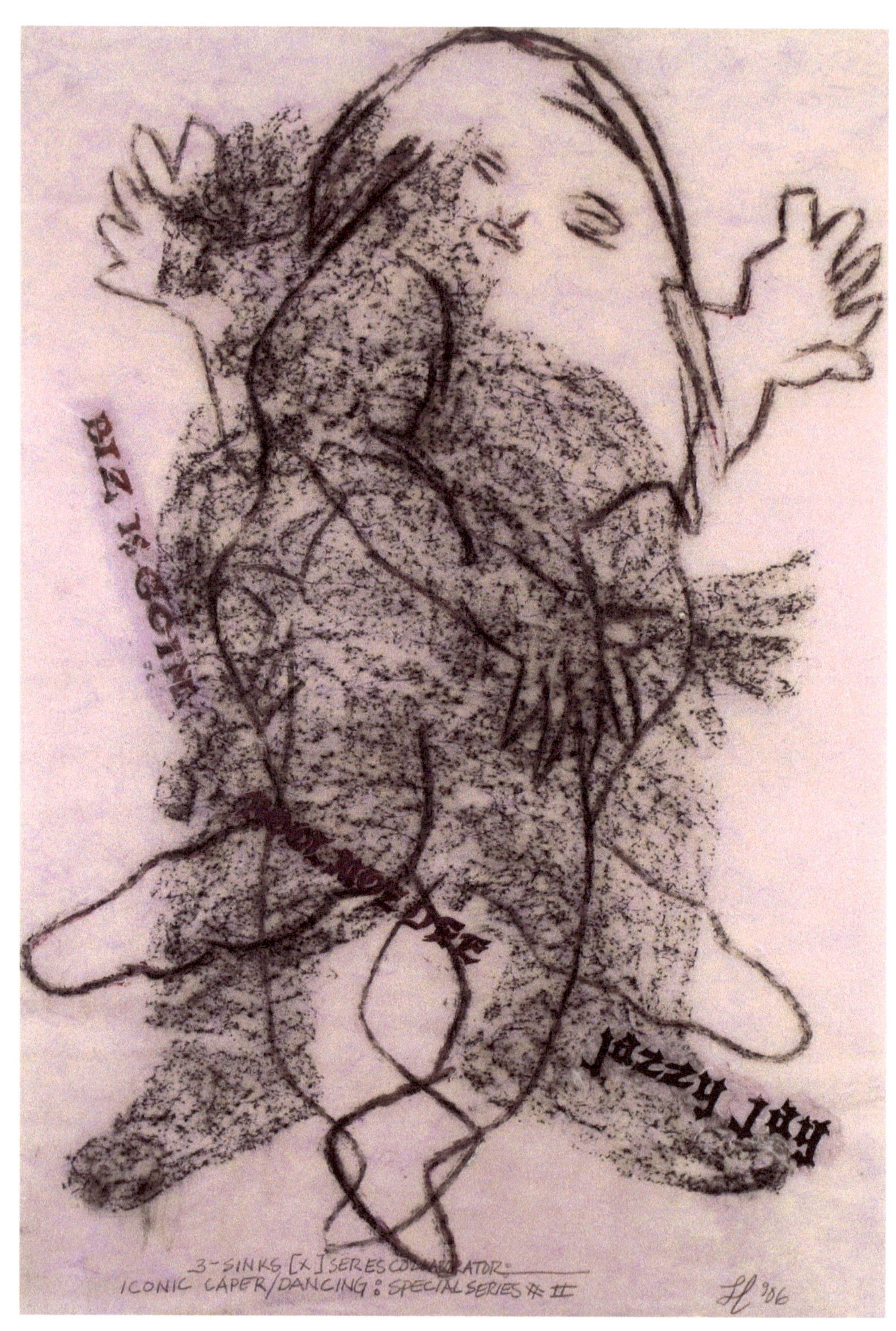

Three Sinks X Series ~ Iconic Caper/Dancing: Special Series #II, 2006

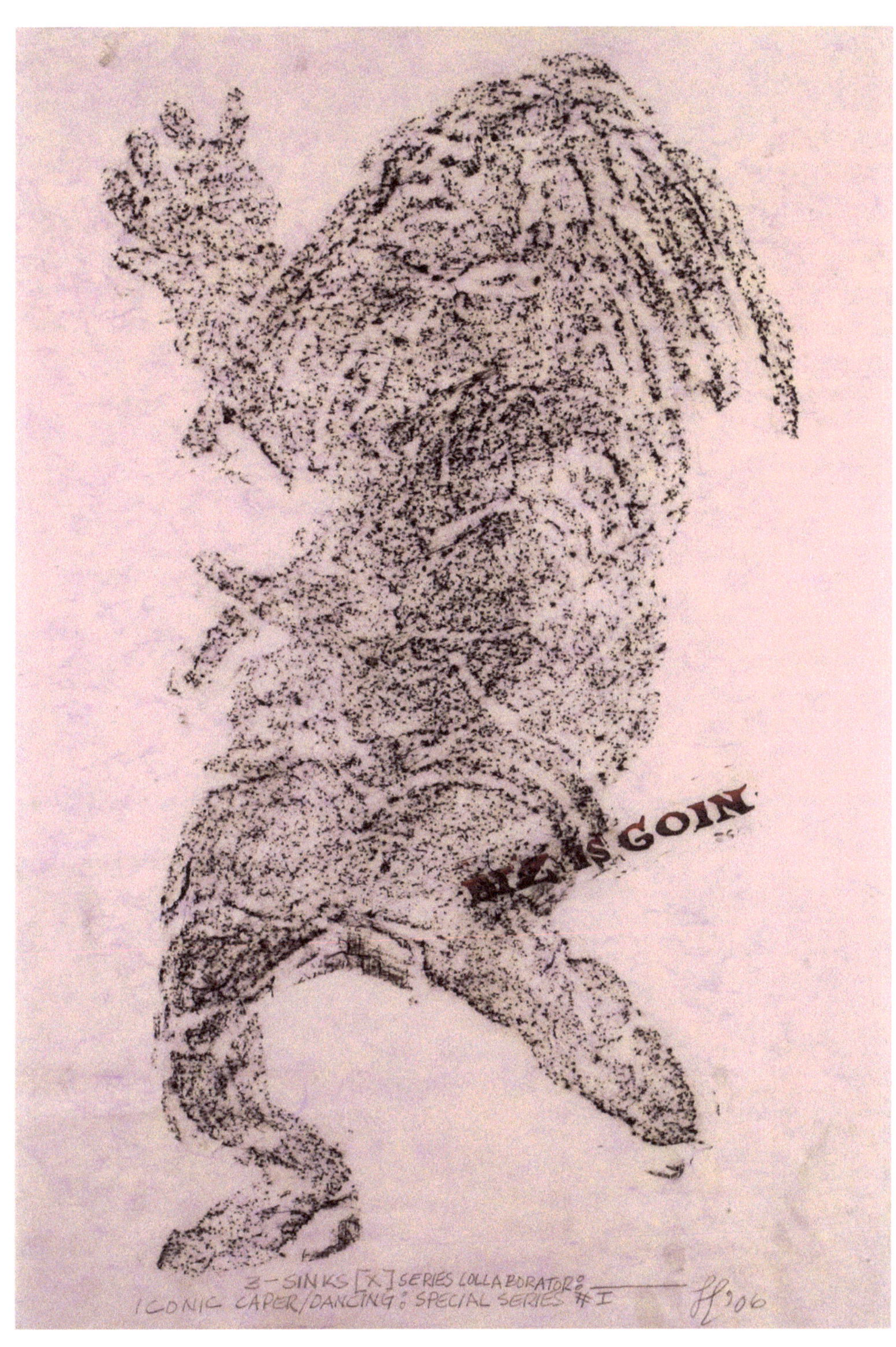

Three Sinks X Series ~ Iconic Caper/Dancing: Special Series #1, 2006

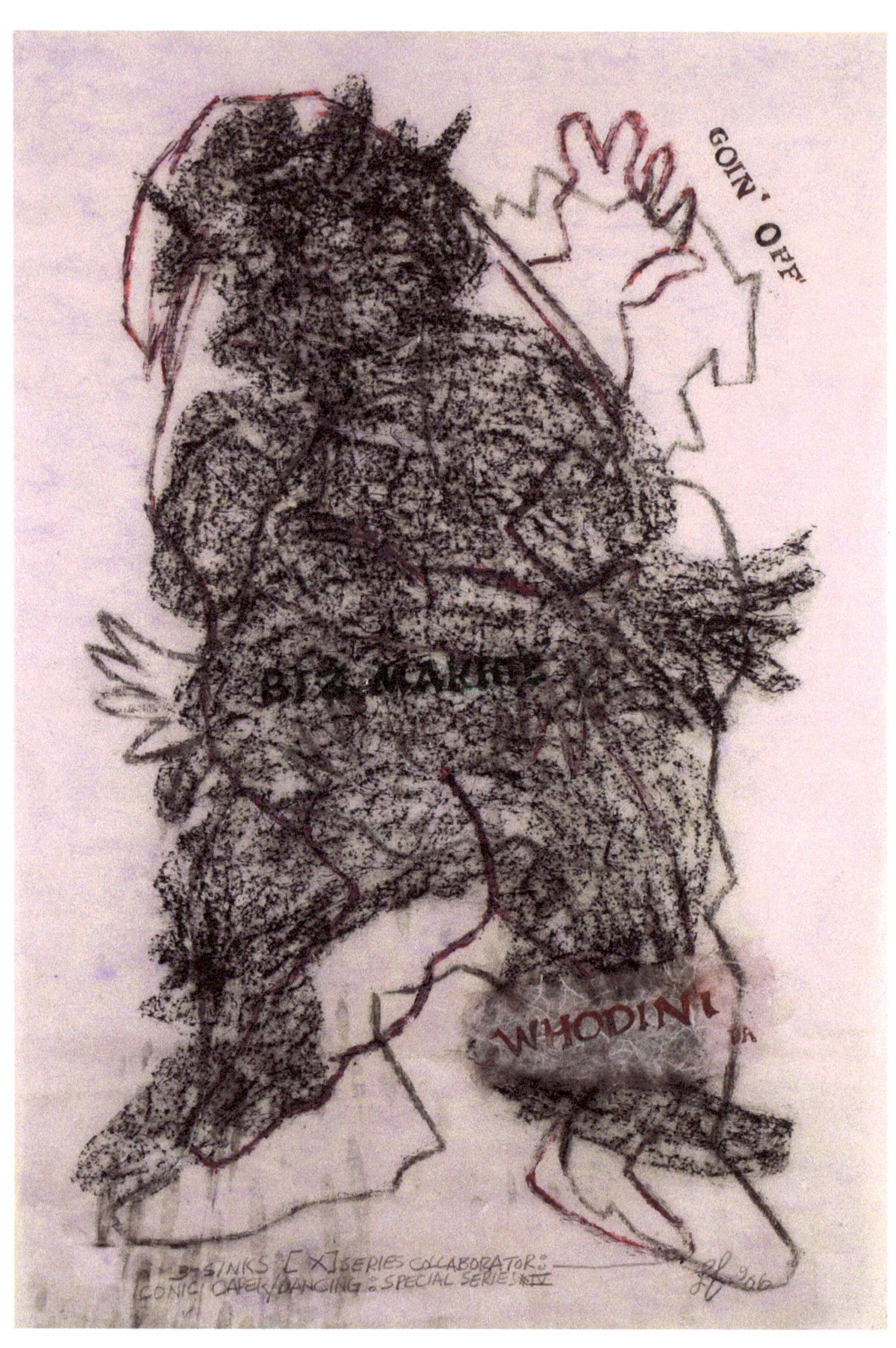

Three Sinks X Series ~ Iconic Caper/Dancing: Special Series #IV, 2006

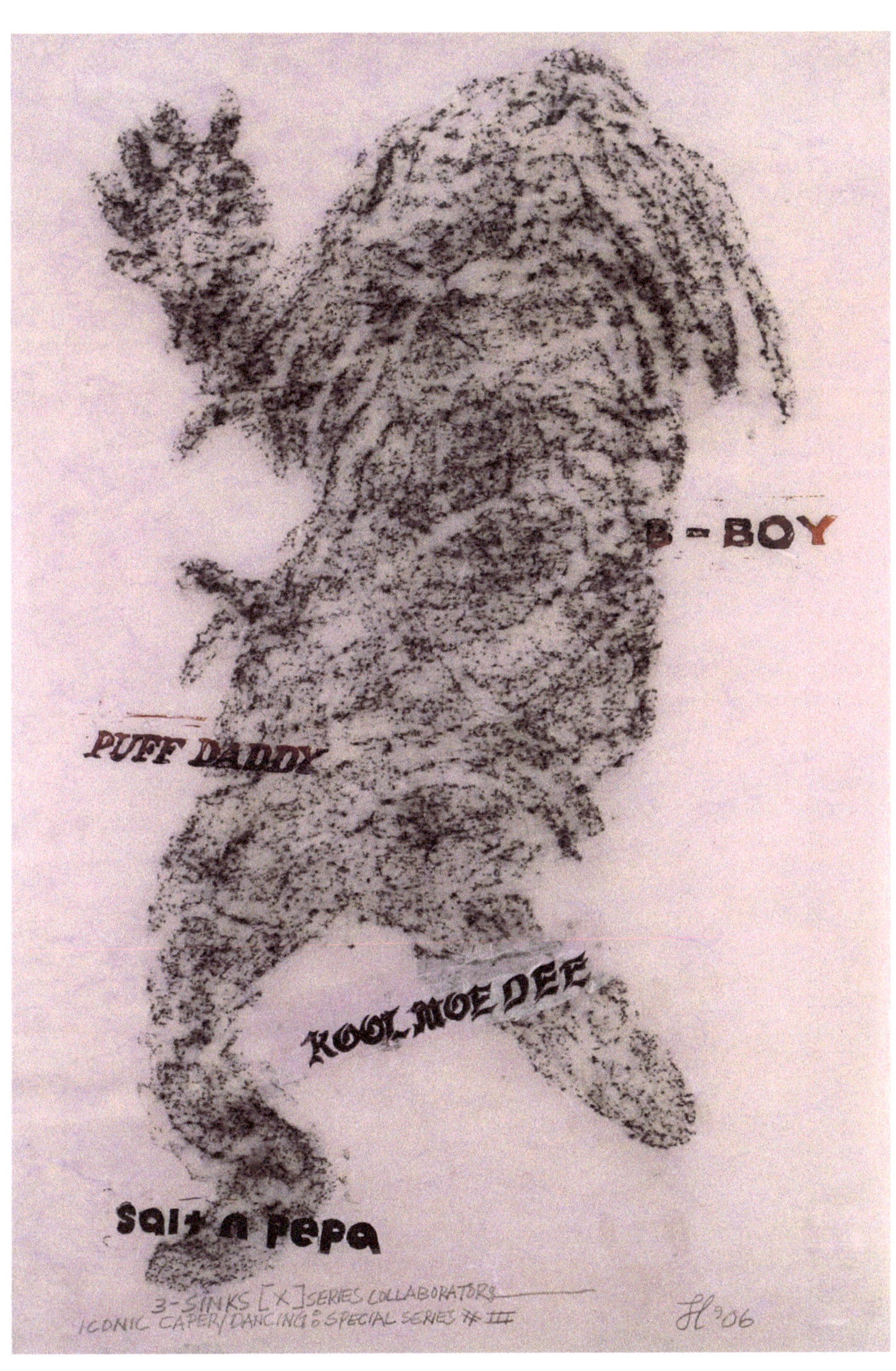

Three Sinks X Series ~ Iconic Caper/Dancing: Special Series #III, 2006

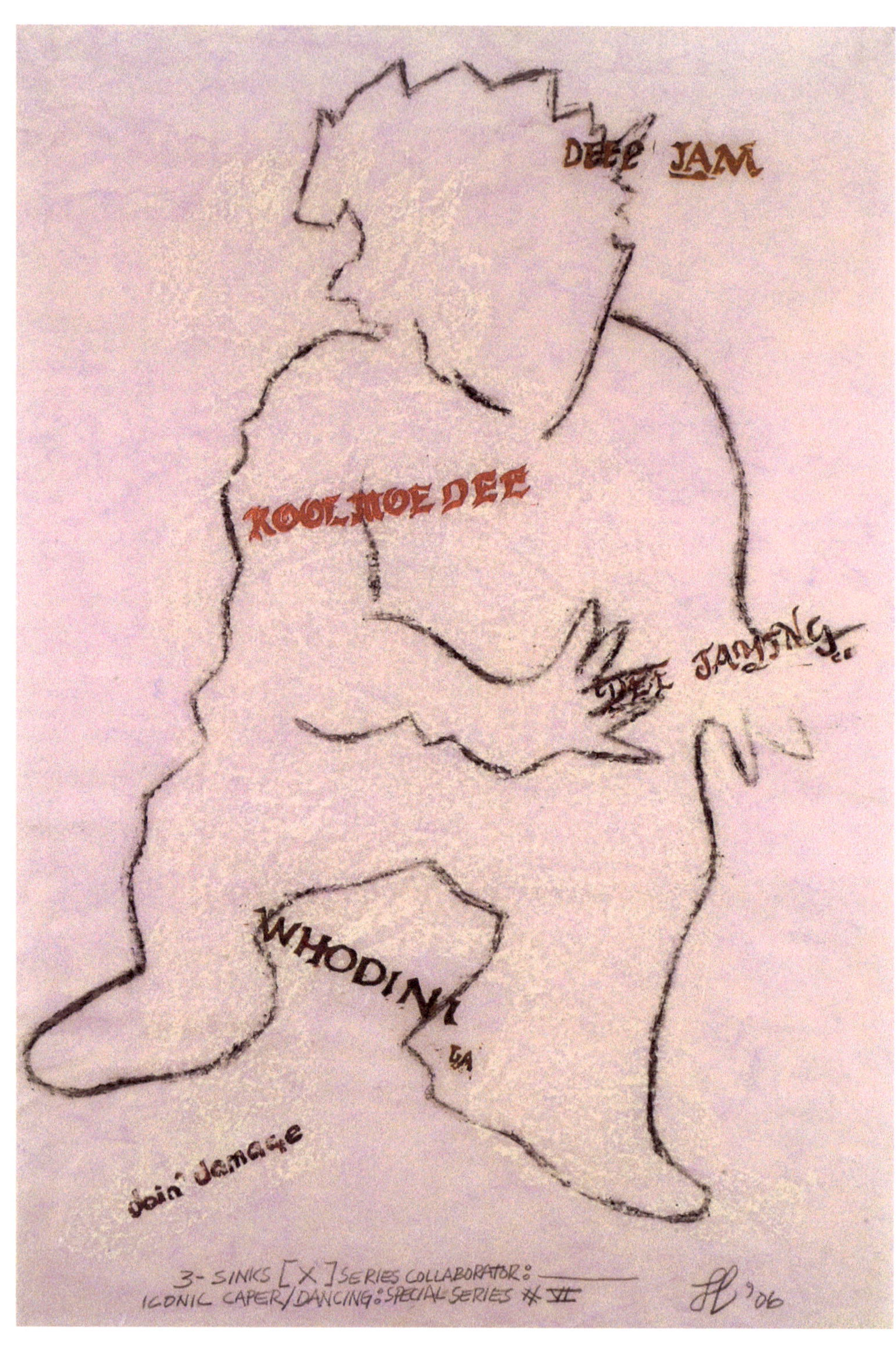

Three Sinks X Series ~ Iconic Caper/Dancing: Special Series #VI, 2006

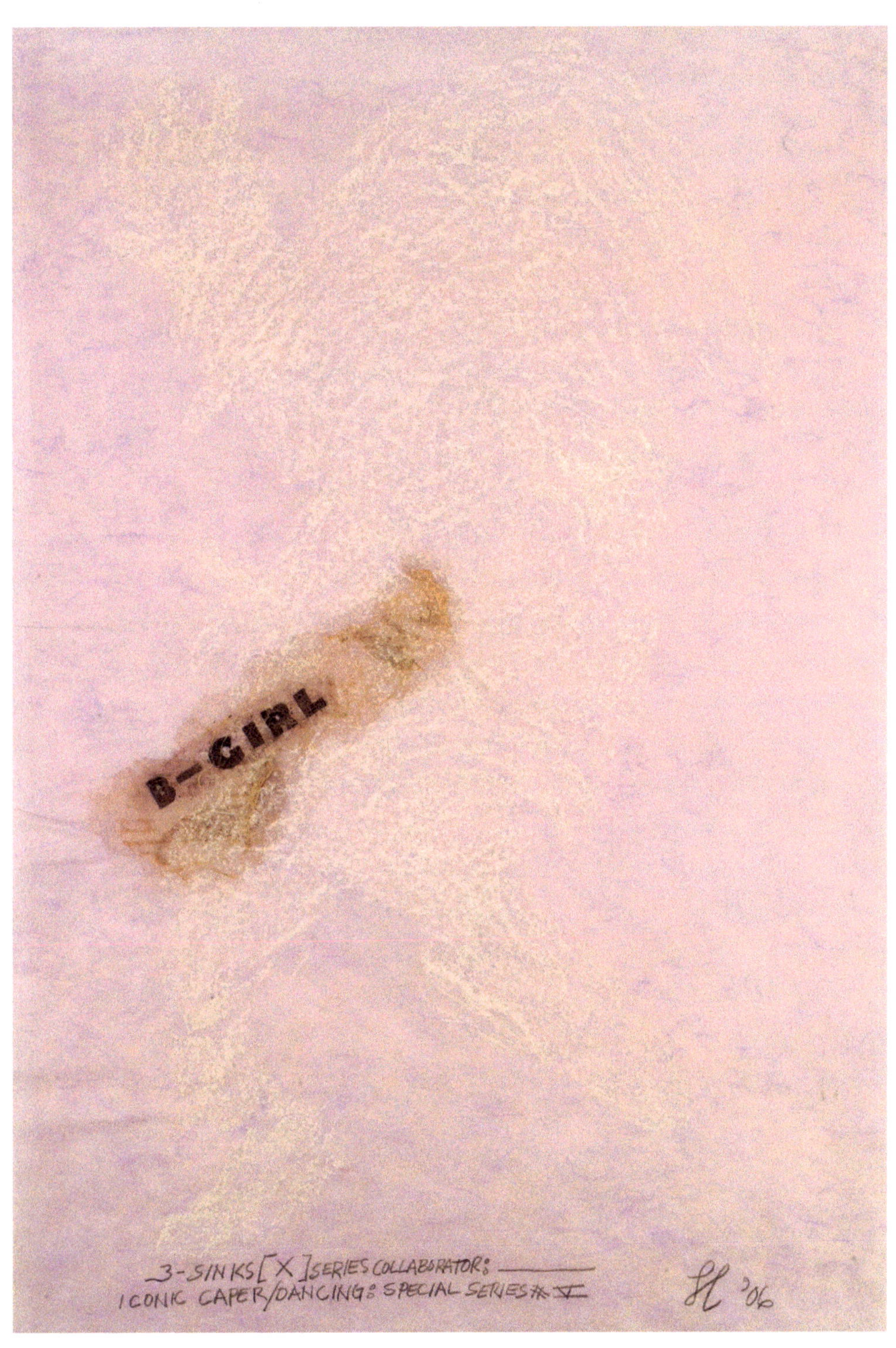

Three Sinks X Series ~ Iconic Caper/Dancing: Special Series #V, 2006

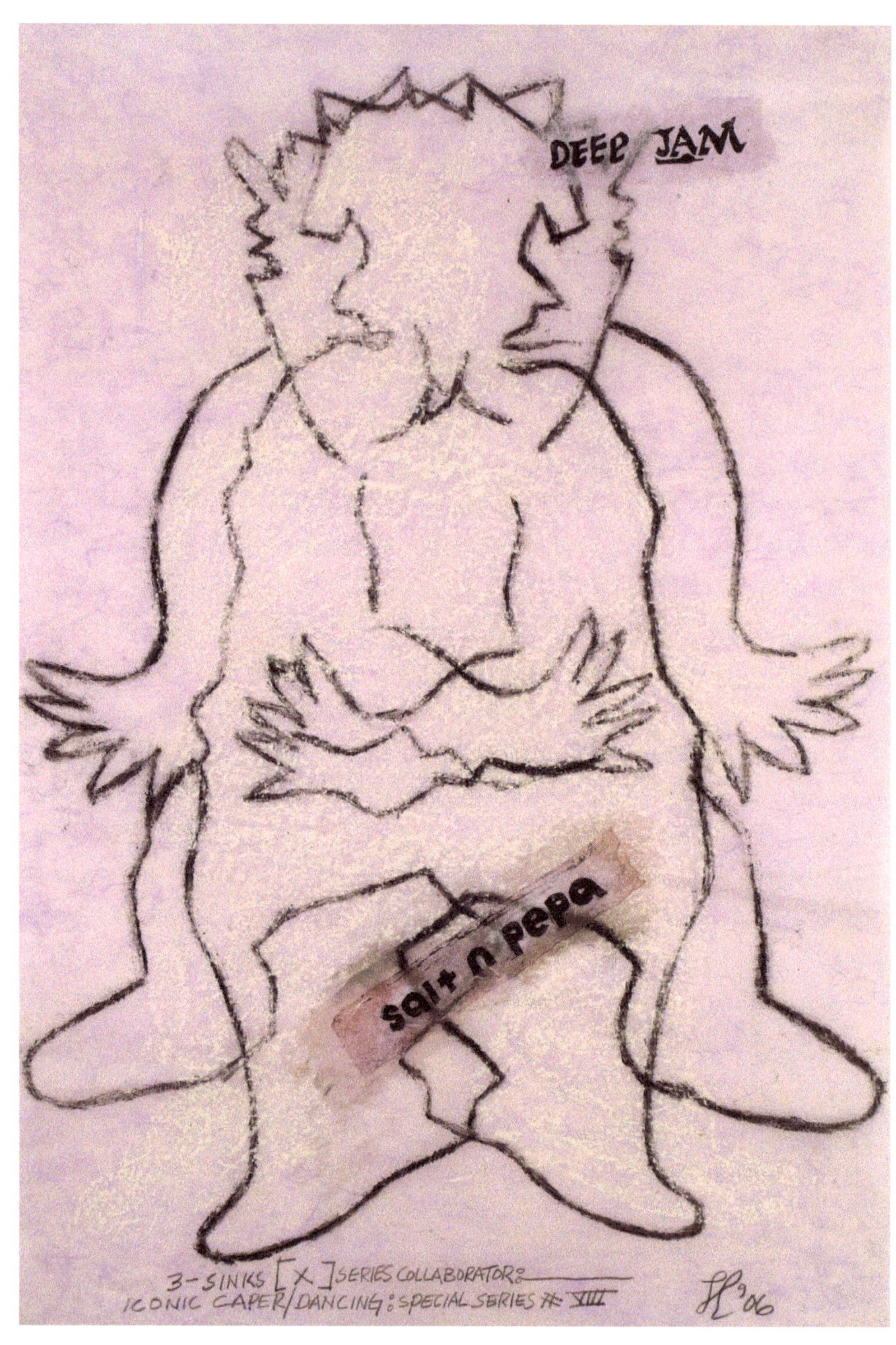

Three Sinks X Series ~ Iconic Caper/Dancing: Special Series #VIII, 2006

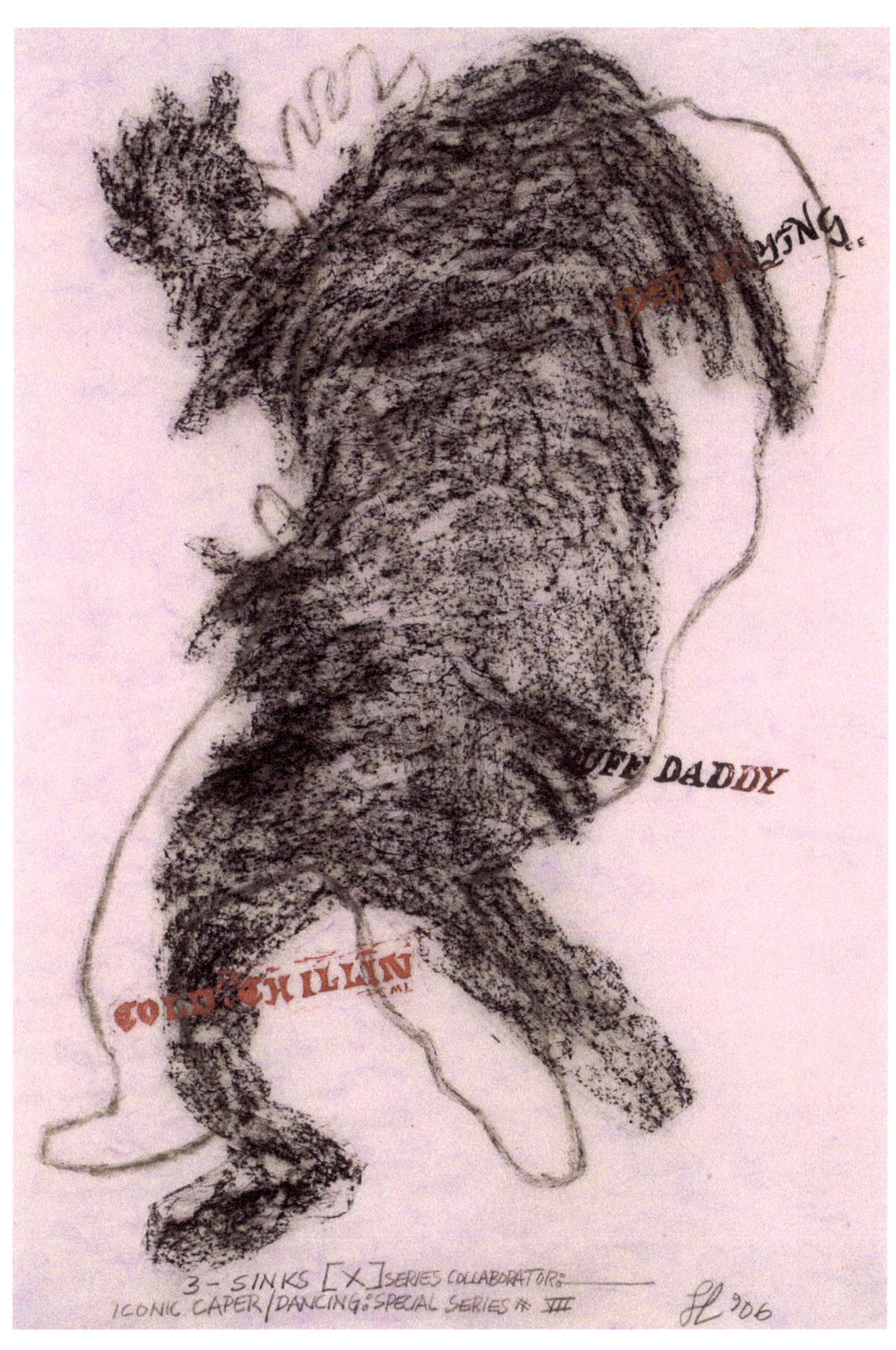

Three Sinks X Series ~ Iconic Caper/Dancing: Special Series #VII, 2006

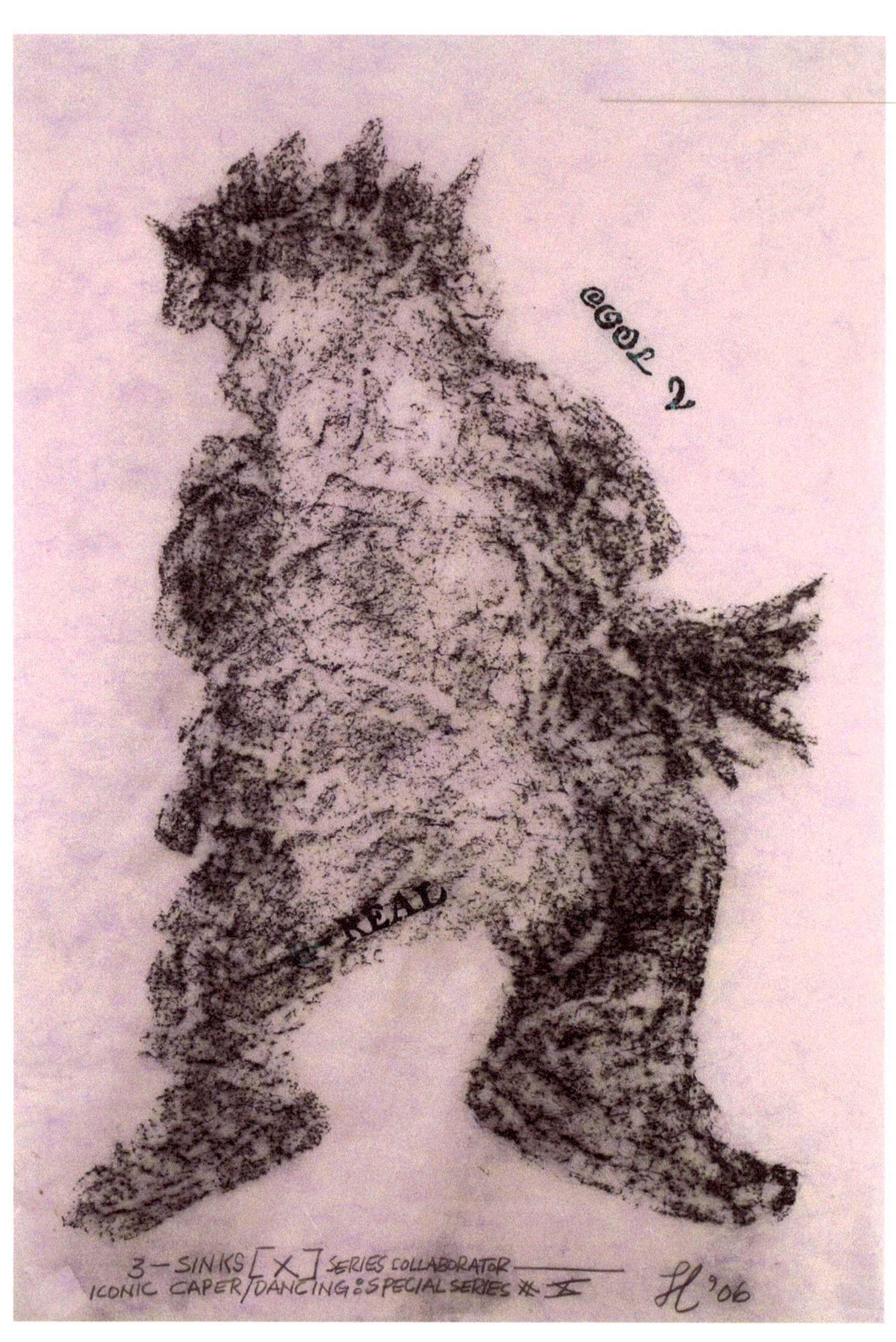

Three Sinks X Series ~ Iconic Caper/Dancing: Special Series #X, 2006

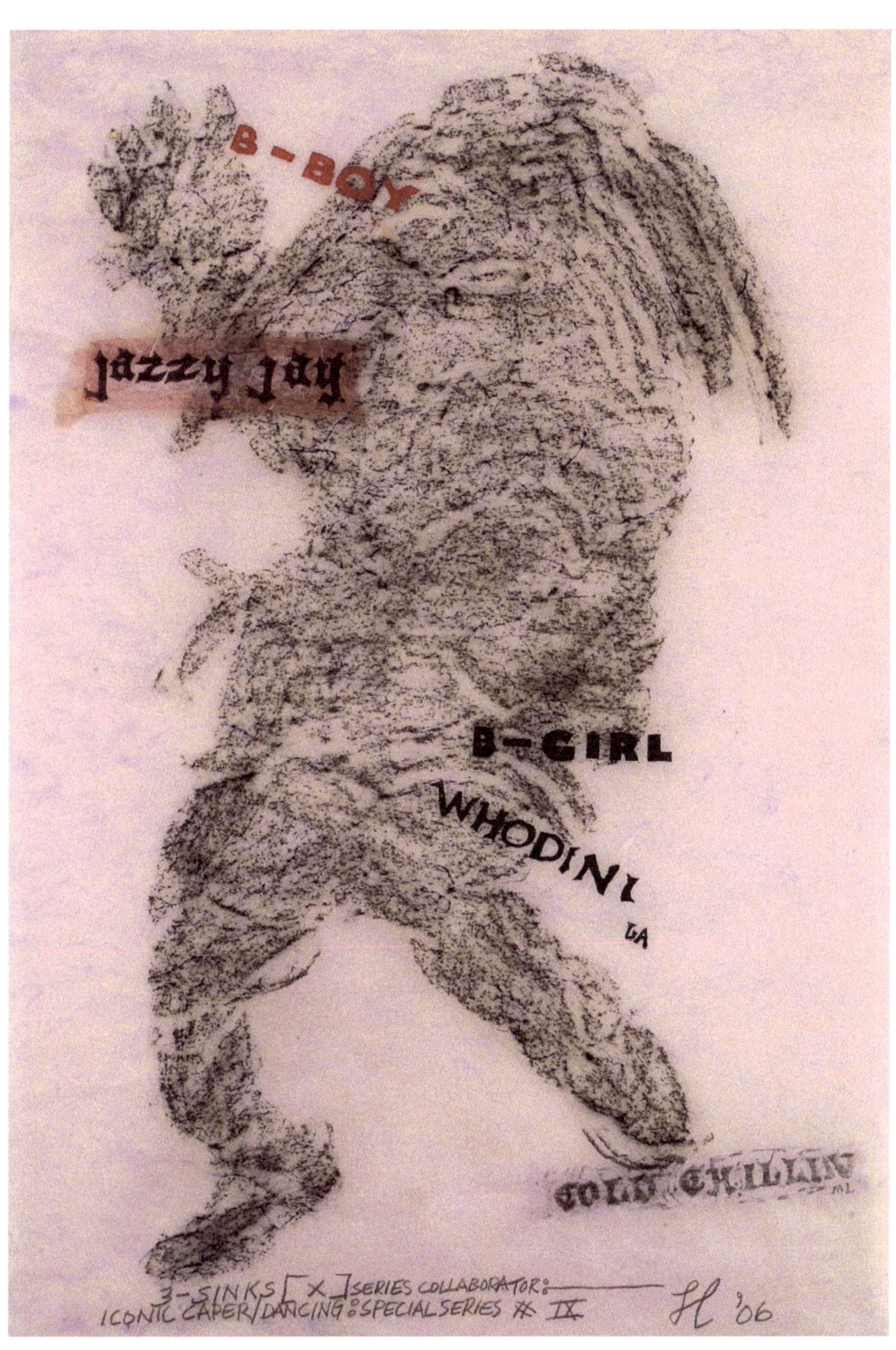

Three Sinks X Series ~ Iconic Caper/Dancing: Special Series #IX, 2006

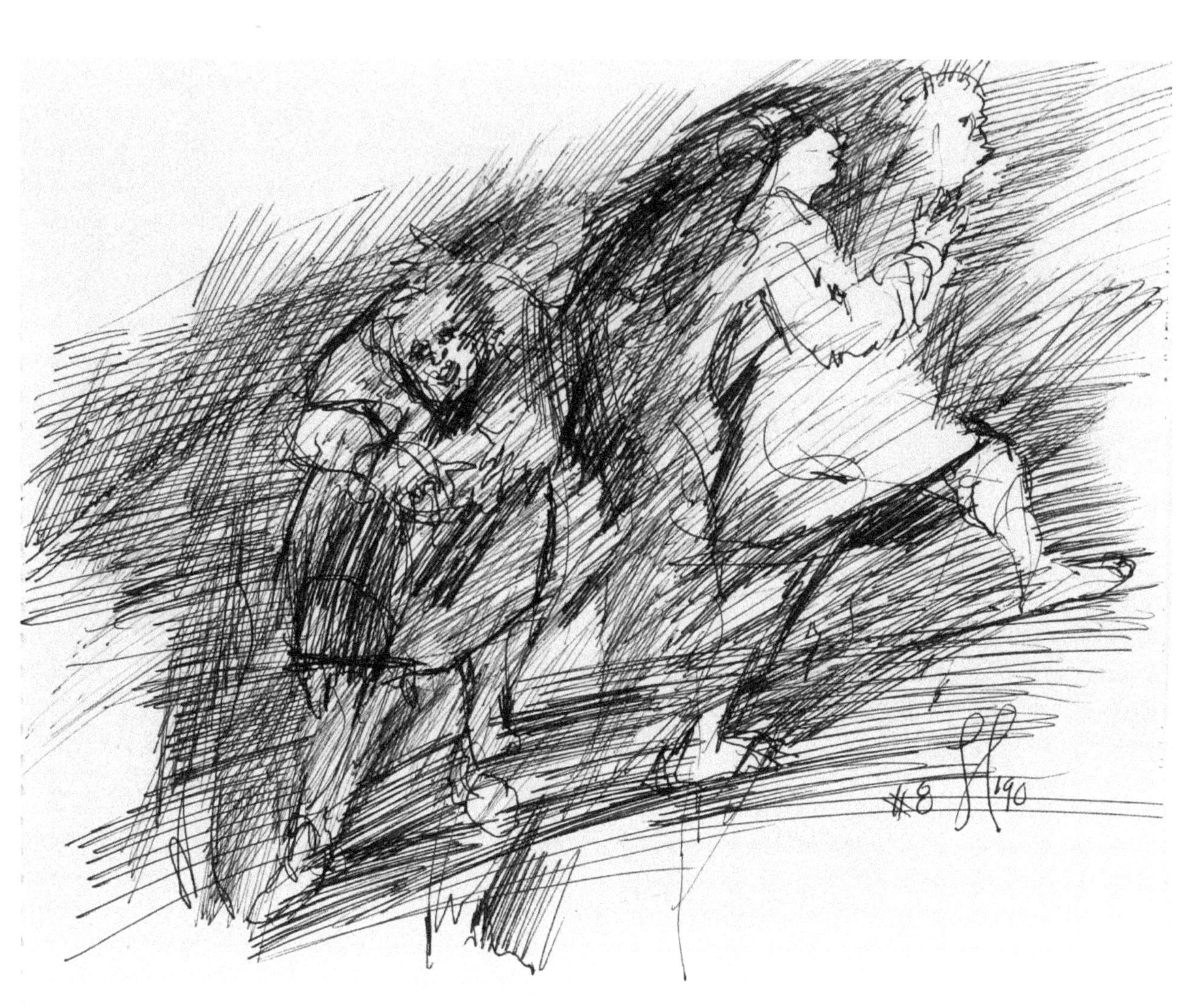

Untitled (Small Line/Mass Pen and Ink Figure Drawing) #8, 1990

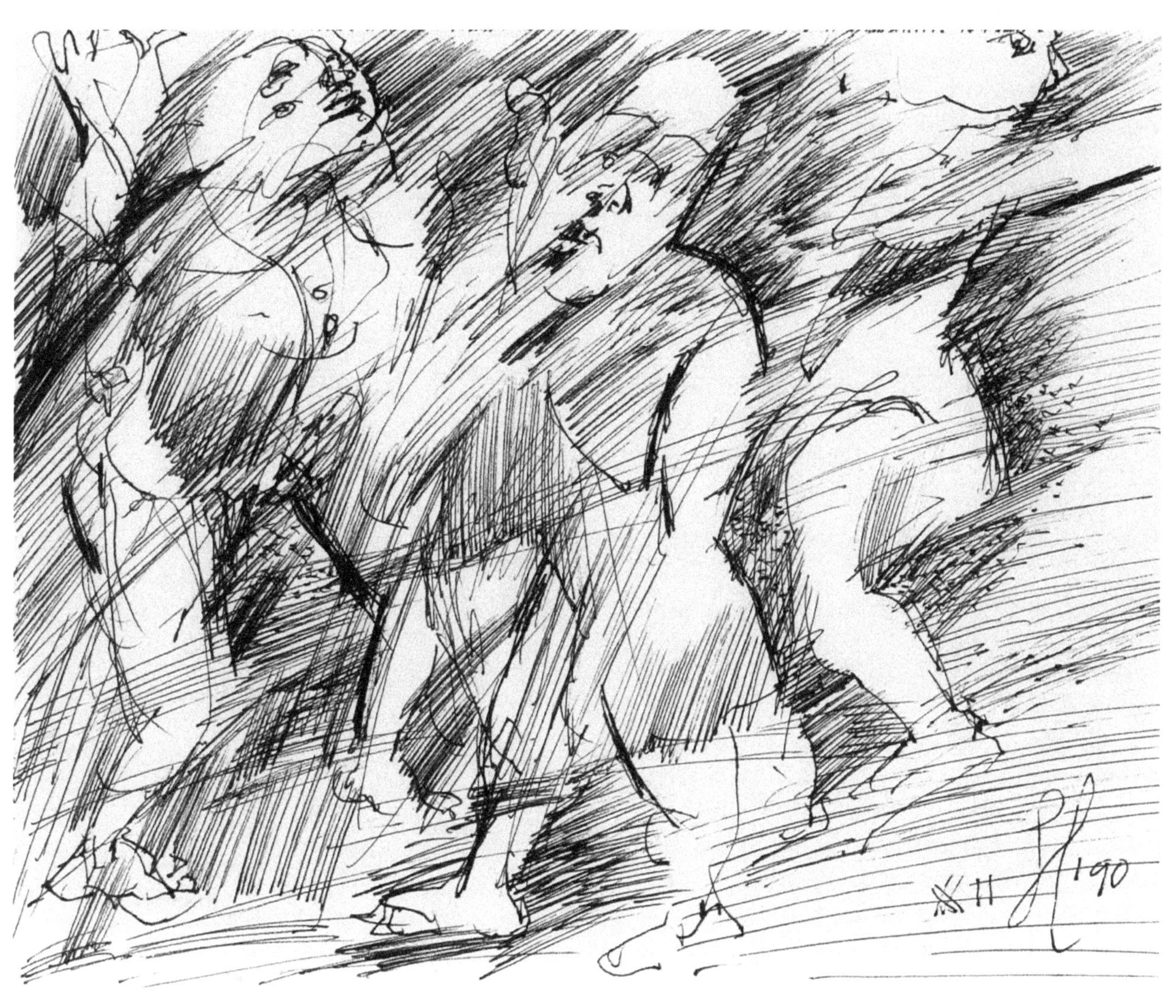

Untitled (Small Line/Mass Pen and Ink Figure Drawings) #11, 1990

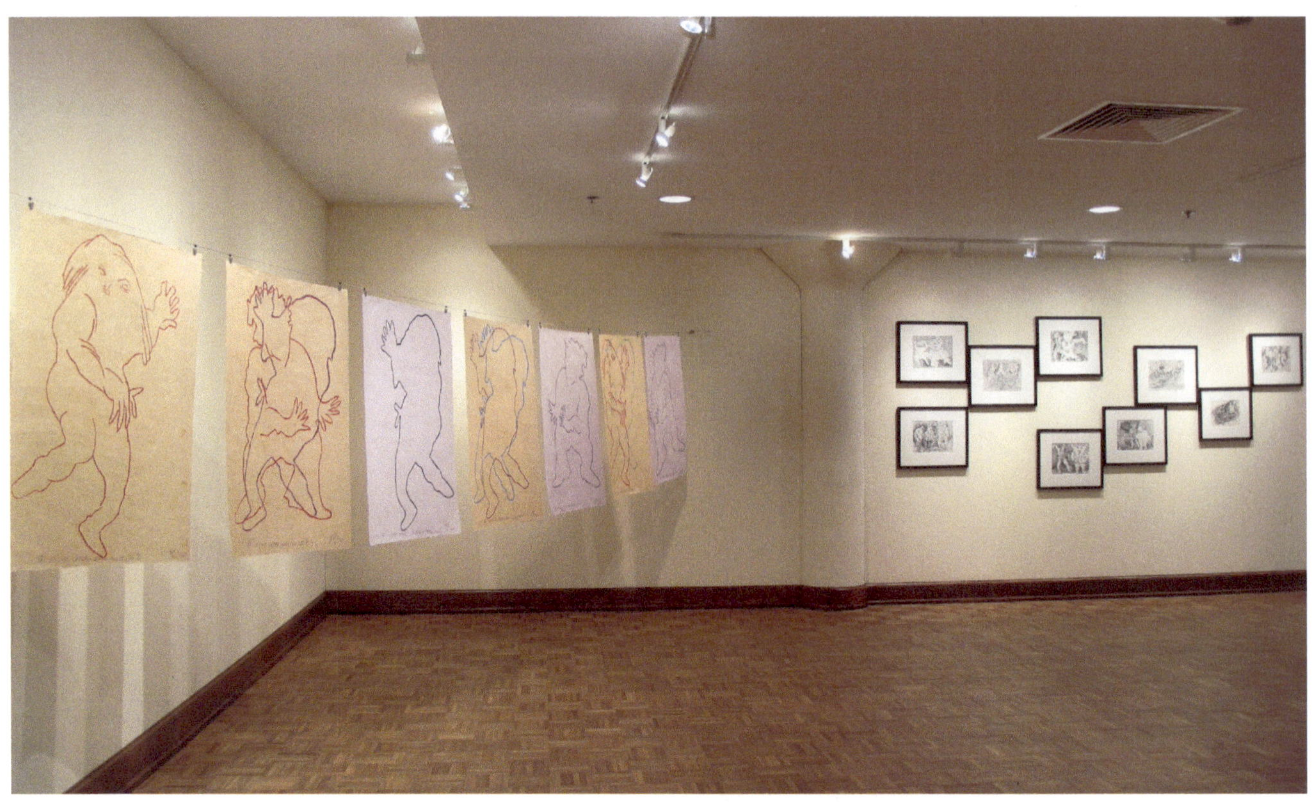

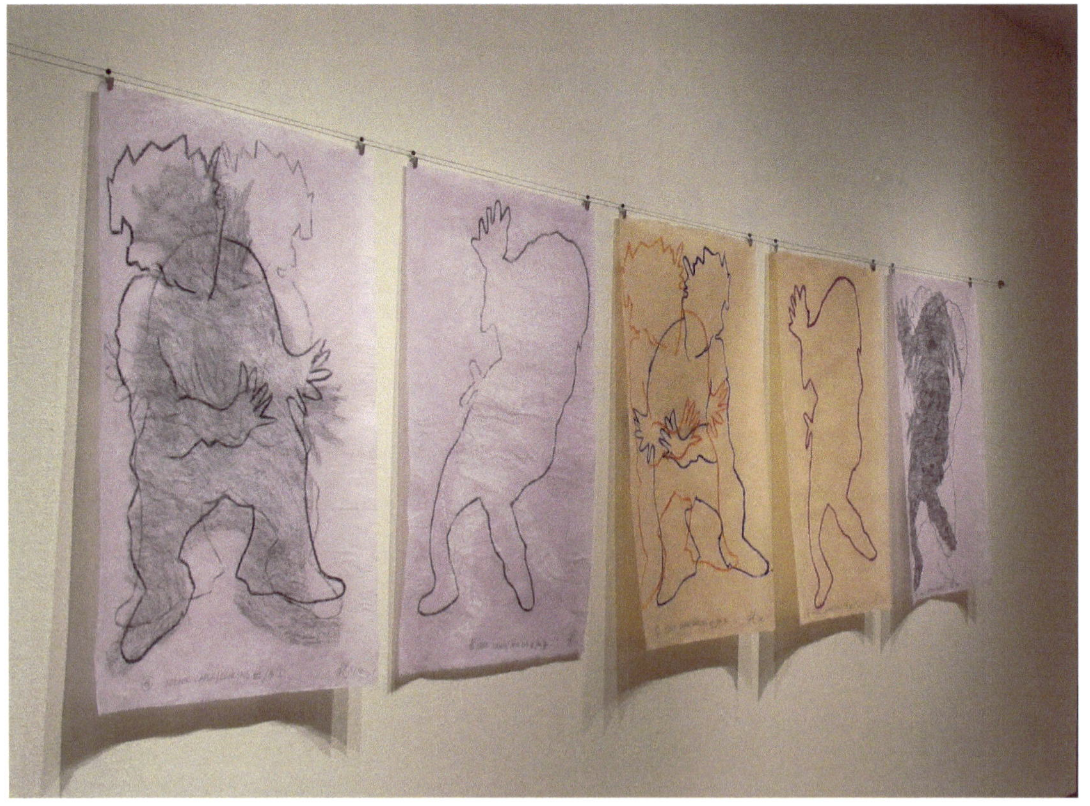

Installation view of *Leon Hicks: Iconic Caper/Dancing* at the Sheldon Art Galleries.

Checklist

Iconic Caper/Dancing Series

A Iconic Caper/Dancing I #1, 2006
B Iconic Caper/Dancing I #2, 2006
C Iconic Caper/Dancing I #3, 2006
D Iconic Caper/Dancing I #4, 2006
E Iconic Caper/Dancing I #6, 2006

A Iconic Caper/Dancing II #1, 2006
B Iconic Caper/Dancing II #2, 2006
C Iconic Caper/Dancing II #3, 2006
D Iconic Caper/Dancing II #4, 2006
E Iconic Caper/Dancing II #5, 2006
E Iconic Caper/Dancing II #5, 2006 (alternate)
F Iconic Caper/Dancing II #6, 2006
G Iconic Caper/Dancing II #7, 2006
H Iconic Caper/Dancing II #8, 2006

A Iconic Caper/Dancing III #1, 2006
B Iconic Caper/Dancing III #2, 2006
C Iconic Caper/Dancing III #3, 2006
D Iconic Caper/Dancing III #4, 2006

A Iconic Caper/Dancing IV #1, 2006
B Iconic Caper/Dancing IV #2, 2006
B Iconic Caper/Dancing IV #3, 2006
D Iconic Caper/Dancing IV #4, 2006
E Iconic Caper/Dancing IV #5, 2006
F Iconic Caper/Dancing IV #6, 2006
G Iconic Caper/Dancing IV #7, 2006

All grease pencil and Rembrandt pencil on lavender or peach Japanese paper, each sheet 36 1/2 x 25 1/8 to 37 x 25 1/8 inches. This series is not meant to be shown or installed in numerical order

The Hip-Hop Allegories

Hip-Hop Allegory, C'est La Vie #1, 2006
Hip-Hop Allegory, C'est La Vie #2, 2005
Hip-Hop Allegory, C'est La Vie #3, 2005
Hip-Hop Allegory, C'est La Vie #4, 2005
Hip-Hop Allegory, C'est La Vie #5, 2005
Hip-Hop Allegory, C'est La Vie #6, 2005
Hip-Hop Allegory, C'est La Vie #7, 2005
Hip-Hop Allegory, C'est La Vie #8, 2005
Hip-Hop Allegory, C'est La Vie #9, 2005
Hip-Hop Allegory, C'est La Vie #10, 2005
Hip-Hop Allegory, C'est La Vie #11, 2005
Hip-Hop Allegory, C'est La Vie #12, 2005
Hip-Hop Allegory, C'est La Vie #13, 2005
Hip-Hop Allegory, C'est La Vie #14, 2005
Hip-Hop Allegory, C'est La Vie #15, 2005
Hip-Hop Allegory, C'est La Vie #16, 2005
Hip-Hop Allegory, C'est La Vie #17, 2005
Hip-Hop Allegory, C'est La Vie #18, 2005
Hip-Hop Allegory, C'est La Vie #19, 2005
Hip-Hop Allegory, C'est La Vie #20, 2005

All ink on paper, 9 x 12 inches.

Three Sinks X Series

Three Sinks X Series ~ Iconic Caper/Dancing: Special Series I, 2006
Three Sinks X Series ~ Iconic Caper/Dancing: Special Series II, 2006
Three Sinks X Series ~ Iconic Caper/Dancing: Special Series III, 2006
Three Sinks X Series ~ Iconic Caper/Dancing: Special Series IV, 2006
Three Sinks X Series ~ Iconic Caper/Dancing: Special Series V, 2006
Three Sinks X Series ~ Iconic Caper/Dancing: Special Series VI, 2006
Three Sinks X Series ~ Iconic Caper/Dancing: Special Series VII, 2006
Three Sinks X Series ~ Iconic Caper/Dancing: Special Series VIII, 2006
Three Sinks X Series ~ Iconic Caper: Dancing: Special Series IX, 2006
Three Sinks X Series ~ Iconic Caper/Dancing: Special Series X, 2006

All grease pencil and Rembrandt pencil and ixed media on lavender or peach Japanese paper, each sheet 36 1/2 x 25 1/8 to 37 x 25 1/8 inches. Selection shown at the Sheldon Art Galleries and Three Sinks Gallery, St. Louis.

Untitled (Small Line/Mass Pen and Ink Figure Drawing) #8, 1990
Untitled (Small Line/Mass Pen and Ink Figure Drawings) #11, 1990

All ink on paper, 8 x 12 inches

By request of the artist, the pieces in each series are not meant to be shown in numerical order, but instead each installation is designed by the individual curator of the exhibition.

www.ingramcontent.com/pod-product-compliance
Lightning Source LLC
LaVergne TN
LVHW070142110826
845147LV00002B/310

* 9 7 8 0 6 1 5 1 4 1 0 1 5 *